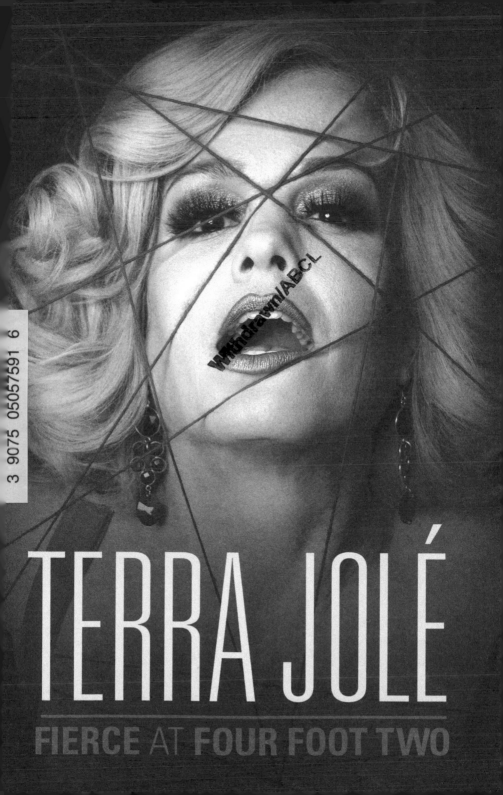

TERRA JOLÉ

FIERCE AT FOUR FOOT TWO

A POST HILL PRESS BOOK

Fierce at Four Foot Two
© 2017 A&E Television Networks, LLC.
All Rights Reserved

ISBN: 978-1-68261-461-7
ISBN (eBook): 978-1-68261-462-4

This work is a memoir. It reflects the author's present recollection of her experiences over a period of years. Certain names, locations, and identifying characteristics have been changed. Dialogue and events have been recreated from memory, and, in some cases, have been compressed to convey the substance of what was said or occurred.

Cover Design by Scott Rohlfs
Interior Design and Composition by Greg Johnson/Textbook Perfect

PRESS
Post Hill Press
New York • Nashville
posthillpress.com

Published in the United States of America

"And though she be but little,
she is fierce."

–WILLIAM SHAKESPEARE

To Mom, Joe, Penelope, D'Artagnan, and Bourn.

This book would not be possible without you.

I love you all so very much.

CONTENTS

ACKNOWLEDGMENTS

I would like to thank the following people (listed in no particular order):

Lifetime for believing in *Little Women* and me!

Roy Rosental for always believing in me and for being the driving force.

Post Hill Press for making this book a reality.

Wenonah Hoye for her editorial direction.

Chris Coelen—none of this would be possible without you.

Dad, I see you visiting me often with love.

Erica Duff you are my right hand!

Tabitha Barnes—thank you thank you thank you.

Larry Zerner, Bob Odmark, Betty Howe, Aunt Julie, Uncle Pat, and Uncle Jerry.

Mrs. BMW (aka Bonnie) the choir teacher who said: "You can!"

Dancing with the Stars and Sasha Farber, for never doubting we could do it.

My publicist, Susan Madore.

Paria Sadighi for highlighting my life.

Tovah Collins, my sister from another mister.

Dr. Danielpour for changing my daughter's world, and our world too.

Dr. Jick: You are the best doctor a girl could ever ask for.

Citizen Cope for music.

Alejandra and Crystal, my life would not be the same without the three amigas!

Leah Smith, though we are far apart, you are in my heart.

Scott Lonker for believing that there was a show before there was a show.

Kinetic Content for taking a chance and being so incredible on this *Little Women* journey.

Eric Detwiler (EP, show runner, therapist, and friend): Thank you!

Ashley Snoddgrass, there are few friends like you. I love you.

Sarah Smith: Keep singing!

Jennifer Lee, for helping put a roof over our heads.

Patricia Gnoffo, the best mother-in-law I could have hoped for.

Scott Rohlfs for the beautiful cover and rocking multiple photo shoots!

Karl Giant for the amazing Mini Britney and Mini Gaga photos.

Adriana for making me beautiful.

Forte Animal Rescue and Animal Defense League.

And a big thank you to the ladies of *Little Women: LA*: Tonya Banks, Briana Renee, Jasmine Sorge, Elena Gant, Traci Harrison, Christy Gibel, and Brittany Guzman.

CLIMB EVERY MOUNTAIN

I have never been one to allow my dwarfism to stand in the way of anything I have wanted to achieve. As a little person (or LP, as we like to call ourselves), I have experienced discrimination and inequality my entire life. I have been told over and over that I couldn't do certain things because of my size, but I refuse to allow anything or anyone to hold me down. While others may see dwarfism as a disability, I have learned to embrace my size and to work that much harder to achieve my goals. So, when the opportunity to climb a 140-foot pyramid presented itself, my immediate reaction was: Challenge accepted.

We were in Mexico filming for Season 4 of *Little Women: LA*, and it was actually on that trip that it hit me for the first time just how popular the *Little Women* franchise had become. At the time, *Little Women: LA* and *Terra's Little Family* were the highest rated shows on Lifetime in all of Latin America, and everywhere we went we were getting recognized from the show. People kept running up to us and shouting "*¡Las Penqueñas Grandes Mujeres!*" and asking "*¿Dónde está Peh-neh-lopé?*" It was so mind blowing to have this feeling of love from fans that transcended language and culture.

Towards the end of the trip, Jasmine (who had joined the cast the previous season and whose family is from Mexico) had arranged for pedicabs to take us through the ancient Mayan ruins of Coba and for us to climb Ixmoja, the second tallest pyramid on the Yucatan Peninsula. For a little person, steps are (at best) physically challenging, but the 122 ancient stone steps leading to the top of this pyramid was a whole new level of pain. They were almost half as tall as the average LP, some of them were loose, and it had been raining all morning so the pyramid was wet and muddy and the steps felt like they were covered in oil. As if that wasn't enough to scare the crap out of you, our guide (Jasmine's cousin) told us that people had actually fallen to their deaths while climbing to the top.

Out of all the other ladies on the show, Jasmine and Tonya made it the farthest, but even they turned back about a quarter of the way up. You would step on a stone that looked stable, only to have it slip out from under your feet and go flying down the side of the pyramid; there's no railing, so if you fall you fall. My arms and legs were shaking and I kept losing my balance, so I was pretty much on all fours most of the way up (meanwhile, all around me there were children skipping up and down the pyramid like mountain goats).

Because we were filming for the show, a camera had to follow me up and thankfully our director of photography (whose full name is Theresa, but who everybody calls "T") volunteered for the job. T joined the crew in Season Two and from day one she has always worn her dark hair slicked back into a bun. It's so tight that I like to tease her that on a clear day I can see my reflection in it. Because she has such a chill energy, T is always a calming presence when we're filming and that day was no exception. She was right there with me the whole way up, like an angel by my side, cheering me on, "I know you got this, Terra. I know you can do it." I just kept focusing on the sound of her voice as I was climbing because in that moment, she was my motivation to make it to the top. I was carrying a big, heavy backpack, and I remember someone telling me to take it off, but by that point I felt like it was the only thing grounding me to the pyramid. About fifteen steps from the top, I heard a whistle blow and an announcement in Spanish, which judging by the fading light I knew must mean they were shutting down the pyramid for the day. No way in hell was I making it that far and not getting to the top, so I chose to ignore the man shouting *"Nadie más. Nadie más,"* and pushed on.

I may have been one of the last people to make it to the top that day, but climbing that last step and reaching the top of the pyramid was exhilarating. It had been such a long, exhausting journey up, but once I reached the top I experienced the most intense sense of joyful accomplishment. Later, T told me that no one had expected *any* of us to make it more than a few steps up, but she knew *I* would make it all the way to the top. That wasn't the first time I had been underestimated by some, and it certainly won't be the last.

Looking down on the world from high atop that pyramid, I began to reflect on my life up to that moment and of all the steps I had climbed to get to where I was that day. As a little person, I'd battled discrimination, ignorance, and prejudice my entire life, and I'd been underestimated and overlooked because of my size more times than I care to remember. And at that moment, after over a decade struggling to carve out a successful career for myself in the entertainment industry and fighting to be taken seriously as a performer in my own right, I had two number one shows on television, I was married to the love of my life, and we had a beautiful baby girl and another child on the way. The journey there had been long and hard, but reaching the top that day I had no doubt that *this* was exactly where I was meant to be.

CHAPTER ONE

GEESE ARE ASSHOLES

When I was born, I weighed 9 pounds 10 ounces and was the biggest baby in the hospital. That was the last time my size would ever be considered "above average." After thirty-six hours of labor my mother ultimately had a C-section because she couldn't pass my oversized head through the birth canal. I came into the world with such severe clubfeet that my mom said it looked like my feet were wrapped around my legs; so right away she and my dad knew I had health issues. But the first real inkling they had how different I was from other babies was when the doctor came to see my mother a day or two into her recovery from the C-section and asked her if she had any short people in her family.

"My grandmother was five feet," she told him.

"No, I mean *extremely* short," he pressed. "Do you have any relatives under five feet?"

My father's side of the family were all five ten or taller. After emigrating from Sweden, they dropped the umlaut in their name, but over there Ödmark is as common as Smith is in the

1

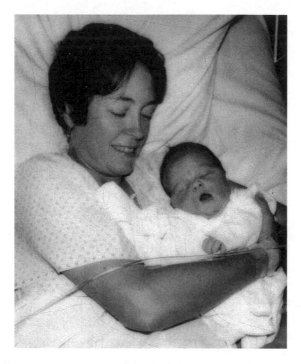

US. My maternal grandmother, Agnes Eaves, was five eleven (with size twelve feet). Her parents were farmers from Norway who had actually booked passage on the *Titanic*, only to be told when they tried to board that they had purchased counterfeit tickets. They ended up having to scrape together what little money they had left to get on the next ship out—which saved their lives. My maternal grandfather, Homer Eaves, was a Native American. His father, Red Cloud (who legally changed his name to George Washington because of all the discrimination Native Americans faced at the turn of the century) died just a few weeks after I was born when he was hit by lightning while driving a tractor on the family farm. My uncle, Vallie "Chief"

My uncle, Vallie "Chief" Eaves, in his White Sox uniform.

Eaves, was a pitcher for the White Sox in the 1930s. It was their mother, my maternal great-grandmother, who was five feet tall.

My mom definitely thought the doctor's line of questioning was odd, but when she told him that we didn't have any relatives shorter than five feet he left it at that, so she did too. She just assumed the reason they kept taking me for tests was because of my feet. Today, doctors generally let clubfeet heal on their own, but at the time they put me in casts to help set them straight, so I spent the first three months of my life with tiny casts on both of my legs. My mother was in the hospital for two weeks recovering from the C-section and on the day she was

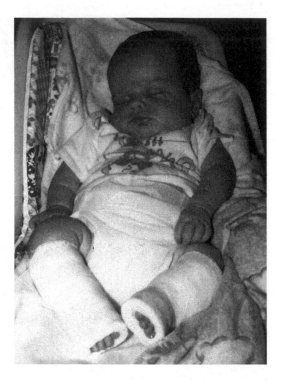

Me (at 3 months) with casts on both my legs.

discharged and getting ready to take me home, the doctor told her that the test results confirmed what he already suspected: that I had achondroplasia, a bone growth disorder that causes the most common type of short-limbed dwarfism. In 1980, expectant mothers didn't have genetic testing or anatomy scans during pregnancy, so up to that moment she had no indication that my development might be different from other children's. The first thought that came to her mind was: *What is she going to do, be in the circus?*

Grandma Eaves was the one who was the most freaked out; she was disappointed and scared for my parents. She knew nothing about little people, and she was mostly worried about how raising a child with dwarfism would impact my parents' lives. My mother's biggest fear was that I would have learning or cognitive issues. The doctor reassured her that during the early years my development might be slow, but that I would eventually catch up—which I did—but that was pretty much the extent of his awareness. Back then doctors didn't know that *all* average-sized parents have a 1 in 30,000 chance of having a child born with dwarfism. Instead they assumed that it must run in the family, which is why the doctor kept asking my mother if she had any "extremely" short people in her family.

Now we know that dwarfism is a genetic mutation. There are over two hundred different kinds of bone or hormone conditions that cause dwarfism, most of which can only be inherited if one or both parents have the same dominant gene—some can't be inherited at all. With achondroplasia, researchers have been able to isolate the gene (FGFR3) to identify and confirm the diagnosis in utero, but there are also definite characteristics: our torsos are of average size, but our arms and legs are shorter; our fingers naturally curve (making it look like we are super *Star Trek* fans); we also tend to have larger heads (the larger the head, the bigger the brain, I always say); and we have bowing in our legs, which gives us our signature waddle. All little people have certain health issues and physical limitations that come with the package, but our hearts and our minds are as big as everyone else's.

||||||||||||||||||||||

I GREW UP IN THE heart of Texas Hill Country. The first six years of my life we lived in Canyon Lake, a sleepy little town just north of San Antonio. It's nicknamed "The Water Recreation Capital of Texas" because most of the town is either on the reservoir or the Guadalupe River. Most of the industry is based around summer cottages, campgrounds, water outfitters, and tubing operations.

My dad was a contractor, and he built a lot of the homes in our neighborhood. After I was born he invested in a couple of acres right on the river and built two houses, one right next to the other. One was a bright yellow, two-story lake house, and the other was a one-story bungalow that was fifty shades of beige; we called them the Big House and the Little House. Between the two houses was a ditch with natural springs, where we used to play all the time when I was a kid; the city eventually filled it with concrete because it was creating a sinkhole. I remember these mounds of dirt everywhere, and if you disturbed them fire ants would come charging out and attack you. We alternated living in the two houses, but mostly we lived in the Big House. There were massive pecan trees in our front yard for climbing and the river just steps from our back porch. Near where we lived there was a bend in the river called the Horseshoe Loop, and on a typical summer day you'd see at least ten people floating down the river from our back porch at any one time. It was a pretty idyllic place for two energetic kids to grow up.

All along the river are wild geese that come up to forage for scraps from the various cottages and campgrounds. My Grandma Eaves lived on the river a couple of miles away in a much poorer area of town. I remember always hugging her leg because she was so tall she seemed like such a giant to me. She was a huge animal lover and every day she fed the geese, even after one of them bit off a link of her finger. Little known fact: Geese are assholes.

Through the hospital my parents were put in touch with Little People of America, an organization that provides support and resources to people with dwarfism and their families. Right away they started going to local meetings once a month. That's where they met Betty Howe, a special education teacher at the local high school who was the Canyon Lake LPA chapter president. Betty and my mom hit it off right away, and they became like sisters. She was a tremendous source of experience and support for my parents over the years, and she ended up being like a second mother to me.

Four days after my first birthday, my brother was born on an army base in New Mexico. He had such serious health issues that he was flown on a jet to a military hospital twenty miles away from us in New Braunfels, Texas. All my mother and father were told was that the biological father was an officer in the military, and that when it seemed unlikely my brother would survive the parents signed over all their parental rights to the hospital in Texas and gave them a DNR order. In addition to having dwarfism, my brother had come into the world upside down, backwards, and he had inhaled amniotic fluid in the womb. No one thought he would survive, but for three months he struggled, clinging to life, in the NICU. When he began to show signs of making it, the hospital reached out to LPA, who in turn contacted Betty about finding him adoptive parents—though, there was no shortage of nurses and doctors who had put their names on the list of potential adoptive parents.

Betty had wanted to adopt him, but in the end she wasn't in a position to take him in. She knew that my mom and dad were planning to have another child, so she told them all about this achon baby up for adoption and how he had survived in spite of overwhelming health issues. My parents felt it was a sign that there was a baby with my type of dwarfism being held a hospital so close by. Without hesitation, they decided to

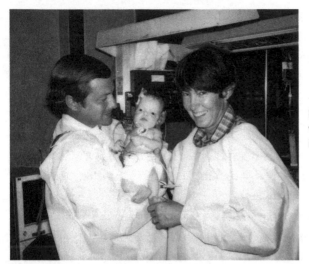

Mom and Dad
visiting Bourn
in the NICU.

Our first Christmas together as brother and sister.

adopt him, and they asked Betty to be our godmother. My mom named the baby Bourn, which means stream or small body of water. (My name means earth.) She gave us names tied to the natural world to honor her Native American heritage.

From the moment he came into our lives, Bourn and I were inseparable. I know it's crazy (because I was barely older than a year) but I have a vivid memory of being at the hospital and looking down into a glass box holding this tiny, doll-like baby with tubes coming out of his nose and stomach. He almost didn't look real, but I knew he was my brother.

||||||||||||||||||||

IT TOOK ME A LONG time to realize that my father wasn't the man that I thought he was. My parents met when they were in their twenties. At the time, my father was an Airman 3.C. in the air force. He had been stationed abroad, but when he started having painful digestion issues they discovered his stomach  was upside down and he had to be shipped back home for surgery. Afterward, to satisfy the balance of his draft requirement, he was sent to Ft. Sam Houston airbase in San Antonio, Texas, where my mom was working as a secretary. The first time they met, he was literally sweeping the floor under her feet. For years they had tried unsuccessfully to have a baby, and they had been married for ten years before I was born. By the time my mother was in her mid-thirties she had pretty much given up on the idea of having children. By then my father was a full-fledged functioning alcoholic and my mother had reached the point where she was seriously considering divorcing him. Then, out of the blue, she got pregnant with me. After I was born my dad seemed to turn over a new leaf. For a time, he was the loving, stable, responsible husband and father that my mom had always wanted him to be, and she fell in love with him all over again.

Richard Odmark and Karolyn Eaves could not have been more different. My dad was a man's man, a contractor who loved his steaks rare and his drinks strong. He was a partier, and he loved to host. He was an amazing cook and whenever he prepared a feast, there would always be a big slab of meat; even his beans would have bacon in them. His main specialty was brisket, which he stubbornly continued to make for me every time I visited him even though I kept reminding him I hadn't eaten red meat since I was eleven. My mom was earthier, with an infinite love for animals and a burning desire to save the

Early photo of my parents, circa 1970.

world. When I was eleven, she had an awakening and became an environmentalist and animal rights activist. I'll never forget coming home from school with Bourn one day to find her crying and throwing out all the meat in the fridge. I was like, "Nooo, not the chicken nuggets!"

She had briefly been a college professor, but she realized early on that she hated teaching and left academia for a quieter life driving a truck for UPS, where she ended up working for almost forty years (when she retired she was honored for over thirty-five years of safe driving), so she could focus on her true passions: protecting the environment and rescuing animals. Because she delivered packages all over Canyon Lake and San Antonio, our mom knew *everybody*. At Christmas our house was always filled with gifts, not for us but for our mom from all the people on her route.

My parents were married for a little over sixteen years, and for some of those years they were happy, that is, when my dad's drinking wasn't getting the best of him. When Bourn and I were little, our mom started getting notices in the mail that our dad owed thousands of dollars for jobs he wasn't completing. She would confront him and they would argue. One of my earliest memories is of being in the living room with my brother and hearing my parents' voices getting louder and angrier. My dad was in the dining room, my mom was in the kitchen, and they were yelling at each other through the cutout in the wall. I can still see the ugly, dark brown and beige vinyl flooring that we were lying on and hear the anger and frustration in my mother's voice. It got so dirty that he was signing her name on documents, dragging her (and, by extension, us) into his messes. But my mom hid all of that from us, so growing up we thought our dad could do no wrong.

My third birthday.

When I was six they divorced and we moved out of the Big House. Our mom bought a place in San Antonio to be closer to the UPS depot where she picked up her truck and all the packages for her route. Our dad moved into an apartment complex about ten minutes away, where he met a woman who had just moved to Texas from Mexico. She barely spoke any English, but within a year they were married. The divorce wasn't so hard for me because I was so young and I still got to see my dad regularly, but it was much more difficult accepting this new woman into our lives because it happened so quickly.

Even after my father remarried he kept drinking, but because he was always functional and never seemed drunk nobody ever called him on it. I remember going over to his apartment when I was a kid and he'd have these purple satchel-like drawstring bags all over the place. They had gold stitching around the seams, and on one side was a fancy gold script that read: *Crown Royal*. I would use them to carry my toys around in or wear them like a purse. I had no clue that all these "fancy" bags were the byproduct of my father's weakness for whiskey.

My mom never spoke to us about what was going on with our dad, so it wasn't until I was in high school that I started to understand how serious his drinking was. After his company went under, he bounced around from job to job and was in and out of rehab. I remember one time, dropping him off at rehab and bawling my eyes out in the car. When he came back a month later, I truly thought he was better, but within weeks he was drinking again. It just turned into him hiding his drinking from everybody. Later on, when I was in my late twenties and living in LA, he began having liver issues. He was supposed quit drinking once and for all. If you asked him, he would say that he quit and that he only drank wine. But when my stepmother would go to the bathroom I would watch him sneak over to the air conditioner unit to take swigs out of a bottle of whiskey he'd squirreled away. I regret not telling my dad that he should stop drinking, or that he was hurting himself, but I always felt that my time with my dad was so precious that I never wanted to spend it being confrontational with him about his drinking.

In the divorce my mom got the Big House and my dad got the Little House, but he never kept up with child support payments so eventually my mom got the Little House as well. He ended up putting my mom in a difficult place because he didn't complete jobs but took the money anyway, so the people he owed money to put liens on both houses. My mom couldn't sell the properties, so she had no choice but to keep renting them out, and she ended up being tied to them for the next fifteen years.

||||||||||||||||||||

FOR AS LONG AS I can remember all I have wanted to do is sing and dance. Growing up we spent our summers up north in Charlevoix, Michigan, with my father's family. We would have these big family reunions with my dad's brother Bob, their sister Julie, and all my cousins. The whole family was musical. Uncle Bob played the French horn, Aunt Julie played flute, and my dad was an amazing oboist. Their father, Clarence Odmark, was a violinist who led the local high school band from 1946–1974. After Grandpa Odie retired, they named the town's amphitheater after him. My Grandma Jan was a high school choir teacher, and she would teach me songs and then, in the evenings after dinner, I would perform for the entire family. I loved having an audience; the compliments and praise I would

Bourn and I going for a ride in our dad's speedboat during our summer visits to Charlevoix.

Bourn and I, playing at Grandma Jan's.

get felt so gratifying. This was before my parents were divorced, so I must have been around three or four, but I knew even then that I wanted to be a performer. I felt like it was in my blood.

When I was five, my parents sent me to a private preschool. At the end of the year the school had a talent show, and I was going to sing "Sandy" from the 1982 film version of the musical *Annie*. I had the perfect little red dress and my mom had learned how to do my hair up in tight little Annie curls; we had choreography worked out and everything. I even had a Sandy, which was one of those battery-operated dogs that walks a few inches, does a flip, and then lands on its feet. I remember rehearsing in the living room and in the middle of the song I did this twirl, and I tripped and slammed my face into the fireplace. My parents rushed me to the hospital, where I got six stiches in my chin. If you're achon (short for achondroplasia) like me, you fall a lot. Most of my achon friends have a similar scar either on their chins or their foreheads. It must have something to do with our center of gravity, and the fact that with our shortened limbs it's harder to catch ourselves when we fall. I've had to get stiches in the same spot on my chin four different times—the most was thirteen stitches.

On the morning of the talent show my mom sat me down and said, "I'm so sorry, honey, but I'm afraid the show's been canceled."

But—I was all ready to go with my little red dress, my hair all curled, and my dumb dog that did flips.

"Why, mommy?" I asked.

"Because it's raining," she answered.

I looked out the window and not a single drop was falling from the sky.

"It's raining *there*, not here," she said firmly.

It wasn't until years later that my mom told me what had really happened. Apparently, the school had decided it was best I didn't perform because they didn't want me to be made fun of for being different; they didn't think the other children would understand my "situation." My mom argued back and forth with them about it, but the school wouldn't budge. So she was left with a heartbroken little girl who couldn't understand why she wasn't getting to perform the song she'd been working on so intensely that she split her chin open doing a twirl. What amazed me when my mom told me this story was the fact that it wasn't the kids at the school who had an issue with me being different, it was the adults who were in charge of "educating" those children who couldn't see past my size.

After my parents split up and we left Canyon Lake, our mom pulled us out of that private school and enrolled us at Northwood

Elementary in San Antonio. I remember that first day so vividly because that was the day I first became aware that I was "little." I'd never been to a public school and I was nervous because I didn't know anyone. We were sitting in these rows of connected desks, and the chairs were slippery so I was having a hard time sitting all the way up. I remember the teacher standing at the front of the classroom and explaining the rules to us.

"Children," she said, "you must sit up straight with your hands on your desks and your feet on the ground. If you have a question during class you must raise your hand to be called on."

Immediately, a boy sitting in the row next to me raised his hand.

"Yes, Clayton," said the teacher.

He looked at me and said in the most timid voice, "But, Miss, this little girl *can't* put her feet on the ground."

The whole class was looking at me and I could hear some kids giggling, before the teacher shushed them. I remember looking around at all the other children in the room, trying to understand why it was that *their* feet could touch the ground but *my* feet were dangling. Later, the teacher pulled me aside and told me she could put a stool under my seat because my legs kept going to sleep.

||||||||||||||||||||

I NEVER DID ASK MY mom *why* my feet didn't touch the floor. We never had "the talk." Mom was always waiting, and she was prepared for it, but the question never came. Recently she said to me, "I was always expecting to one day hear the question, but I never did. Not from you or your brother." I think I just wasn't ready to accept who I was, so if I didn't say it out loud then it wasn't real.

Other than my brother, I didn't really know any little people my own age. We grew up going to local Little People of America meetings every month, and before we moved to San Antonio my parents used to host chapter meetings at the Big House, but I never *felt* like a little person. The LPs at our local meetings were all adults, and growing up I'd look at them and think: *I don't look like them. I don't waddle when I walk like they do.* If Bourn and I were out with our mom, people would make comments like, "Oh, they're so adorable" or "Are they twins?" Never did I hear, "Oh my gosh, they are so *small*," or, "Why do you look like that?"—until I was much older. But if we went out with Betty, who was achon like us, people would stare at us or they would assume *she* was our mother. That's when I became self-conscious of our size and I would feel ashamed and embarrassed.

When I was fourteen our mother took Bourn and me to our first national LPA conference. My parents convinced me to go, but I didn't want to. By then I knew I was little, I just didn't think I was little like *them*. I was still very much in denial. I remember walking into the lobby of the hotel in San Antonio where the convention was being held and feeling like my feet had turned to concrete. I just stood there, staring at everyone. It was honestly the weirdest experience to be looking at so many other people at eye level. At that point, I hadn't even been to a regional meeting (where you'd have a gathering of three hundred little people), so I went from chapter meetings with twenty to thirty members to 1,800 little people looking me right in the eye.

I remember going out to eat that first night at the hotel restaurant, and there were little people with dozens of different types of dwarfism at the tables all around us. Imagine growing up in a world where you are different from everyone else around you, and you *know* that you are different from everyone else, but you've never really met anyone like you before. Then one day, you find yourself eating dinner at the San Antonio Marriott surrounded by hundreds of people who look just like you, and move just like you, and for the first time in your life you feel like you belong. *That* is what it's like going to your first national LPA conference.

It was a quiet dinner because Bourn and I were still just digesting it all. During national conferences, there's usually a dance held every night in the hotel banquet hall from 9:00 p.m. to 1:00 a.m., so after dinner we decided to check it out. There was a DJ, lights, a dance floor, and everything; it reminded me of a wedding reception or a prom. I remember being at the dance, still not really talking to anyone, and a kid my age came over to me.

"I like your shoes," he said.

"Thanks," I said.

Now, this may seem like an insignificant moment to most people, but it was life changing for me. Other than my brother, I'd never talked to another little person *my age* before. He asked me to dance, and that night was the most fun I had ever had in my entire life at that point.

At national LPA conferences, there are different events throughout the week that go on every night. There are fashion, talent, and comedy shows, all kinds of sporting events and competitions, and an awards banquet at the end of the week. As a little person, you finally feel like it's a level playing field. It only took me that first day to get over the hump; from there I was hooked. That year, I sang a duet with Bourn from *My Fair Lady* in the talent show and Bourn joined the basketball team. He'd always wanted to play sports, but until then our mom had

Me and Bourn with Billy Barty, the founder of Little People of America (1994, San Antonio conference).

made him stick to golf because she was so worried he'd get hurt. We both made tons of friends (some of whom are in my life to this day), and I didn't want it to end. For the first time in my life I felt "normal." Our mom promised she'd take us to the convention in Denver the following year, and she did. LPA sends out quarterly newsletters and after a conference there are always tons of photos from the various events. I remember checking the mail every day and then, when the newsletter finally came, excitedly scanning every single page for photos of me and my friends.

It was *that* moment on the dance floor of my first national LPA conference, dancing with the boy who had complimented my shoes, that I finally began to find myself—even though I hadn't even fully realized I was lost. The boy and I kept in touch a bit over the years and when he was in his twenties he elected to have a very painful limb-extension surgery to give him an extra foot of height. I don't know if he ever quite came to terms with being a little person. I heard a few years ago that he had passed away from an overdose of medication.

CHAPTER TWO

IF YOU CAN'T GET PAST MY SIZE, YOU'RE THE ONE WHO'S SMALL

All I wanted going into middle school were a pair of Girbaud jeans and a JanSport backpack. We didn't have a lot of money growing up, and my mom flat-out refused to buy me the designer jeans, but she did buy me the backpack. I was so excited, but then on my first day of sixth grade this shitty kid pushed me up against the lockers and stole it from me. I told a teacher and she searched the backpack, but there was nothing in it that proved it was mine so she said there wasn't anything the school could do about it. The worst part was that I saw that kid a week later with a different backpack. He didn't even want mine; he had just taken it to show off to his friends. For my mom to buy me that brand-name backpack and then have some kid steal it from me less than a week later was devastating. I was so nervous to tell her what had happened and when I finally did all she said was, "Well, I'm not buying you a new one." I had to use a crappy grocery store backpack for the rest of the school year. I did eventually save enough money to buy myself a pair of Girbaud jeans I found on clearance—they had red and white stripes, which explains why they were on clearance.

Bourn had a much harder time in school than I did. Kids would call us "midget" to try to get a rise out of us and impress their friends. Although I'd pretend I didn't hear (and then cry later when no one was watching), my brother would always say something back and then get into a fight—and a little person getting into a fight with an average-sized person is never a good thing. Gym class and the cafeteria were the worst places for us because there's not as much adult supervision. I remember one time this kid kept patting Bourn on the head. He told the kid to stop, and when he didn't Bourn tried to punch him in the head to teach him a lesson. He would never back down and there were a couple of times he got suspended for fighting. Most of the fights he got into were Bourn defending *me*, because I never stood up for myself. Like most siblings, we fought like cats and dogs, but beyond being brother and sister, we also had the bond of being different so we were very close. He always had my back.

The best part about middle school was show choir. The teacher, Miss BMW, taught us solfège, a method of teaching singers to sight-read music using the do-re-mi syllables, which was unusual for a middle school choir teacher. We all loved Miss BMW, and when she got married (and changed her name to Mrs. BMC), she invited our show choir to sing "Chapel of Love" at her wedding. In eighth grade we went to Houston for our big competition and Mrs. BMC gave me a solo part in "I Will Follow Him." She didn't tell me they were giving a separate award for soloists because she didn't want to make me nervous, but lo and behold I won first place for middle school soloist at

My mom and I
before a show
choir recital.

the competition. I still have that trophy. It's beat up and rickety now, but I've kept it all these years as a reminder of the first time someone truly believed in me as a performer.

Middle school was rough at times, but by high school I had found my groove socially. Alejandra and Crystal were my two best girlfriends and we rode the bus to school together every day. Alee and I had met on the bus in middle school and we hated each other all through sixth and seventh grades. Then in eighth grade the bus driver assigned seats next to each other, and after that we became best friends for life. In freshman year, Alee joined the pep squad and I joined the women's choir. Alee met Crystal in pep squad; at first I was jealous that they were becoming friends, but then we all started all hanging out and to this day they are two of my closest friends.

Our favorite pastime was rollerblading and roller skating around Alee's apartment complex. Alee, who is Puerto Rican, was bold and in-your-face then. She would always be up for an adventure and was more than willing to get into trouble with me, where Crystal (who had crazy-curly blonde hair that she flat-ironed straight every single day) was quiet and introverted. Neither one of them could carry a tune, but they were dance queens—which always made me a little jealous. I was never allowed to take dance classes because my mom was too worried about the impact on my body.

Sarah and Ashley were my choir friends. Sarah, who sang alto, was a short and curvy, outside-the-box kind of girl with a quirky sense of style. She always wore the craziest nail polish colors and you might see her with a purse that looked like a banana, but you wouldn't think twice about it because she was always that kind of outgoing oddball. Ashley, a tall brunette with a slender build, was the total opposite. She sang soprano, was very introverted, and always had to look just so. She was in every honors class possible, and it would be crazy to hear her cuss or say anything inappropriate because she was mature beyond her years. She was the friend you were happy to take home and introduce to your parents because they knew when you were with her, you weren't going to be getting into any trouble. I remember at lunch there was the table where all the choir kids sat and the table with all my school bus friends, and

I would always be bouncing back and forth between the two groups.

I also had my work friends whom I hung out with after school and on weekends. At sixteen, I started working in customer service at Drug Emporium, a now-defunct chain of discount drug stores. That's where I met Sam, who was a stock boy. Sam was one of three brothers, military kids who lived and went to school on the army base near San Antonio. From day one we hit it off, and we would hang out at each other's houses every day after work or school. He got along great with Bourn and I got along great with both of his brothers. On the weekends, we would all hang out, tubing down the Guadalupe River, barbequing, or going to the movies. Even though Sam was a full two feet taller than I, he never had an issue with me being little. We talked on the phone every night, we argued like siblings, and we laughed at all the same things. By senior year everyone around us knew we were in love, but us.

||||||||||||||||||||||

SHOW CHOIR WAS WHERE MY heart was and I wanted to learn and grow vocally. Most of the other choir kids hadn't learned solfège yet, so going into high school I felt very advanced. But, where Mrs. BMC had made me feel like I could do anything, my high school choir teacher, let's call her Ms. Crabapple, was very cold. No matter how hard I worked I always got a weird energy from her, but I couldn't quite put my finger on why. (But I will say this about Ms. Crabapple: she always had the best acrylic nails; even her toenails were acrylic.)

Going into sophomore year I auditioned for Premier Choir, the elite all-girl show choir competition team at my high school. I wasn't chosen, but Sarah and Ashley made the cut. Although I was disappointed that I couldn't be a part of it with them, I just kept telling myself, "Don't worry, you'll get it next year." Going into junior year I didn't make the cut again. I was crushed, and I began to wonder if maybe I wasn't as good as I thought I was. I felt very defeated, but even though I didn't make Premier, I was still in the women's choir. I decided, *I'm just going to work my butt off and try again next year*. That year, I dedicated myself to women's choir and by the end of the season we had won tons of awards. Even though it had been a struggle juggling the demands of school, work, and choir, the payoff was that I was able to contribute to its winning season.

At the end of that year I auditioned for Premier Choir again. Since it was a tradition for all the rising seniors in Premier to have a say in the following year's picks, this time Ashley and Sarah would be in the audience. So, even though all the girls were sworn to secrecy, I knew I would get the inside scoop. I'll never forget, after the audition, sitting in my silver four-door Honda Civic and waiting for Ashley in the back parking lot of our high school. When she got into the car, she was sobbing.

"I didn't make it, did I?" I asked, even though I already knew the answer.

"It's so much worse," she said, shaking her head. "I don't even know if I can tell you."

"How can it be worse?" I asked, and then when she couldn't meet my eyes I realized just how upset she was. "Ashley, did you quit?"

She nodded. It took a while for her to get the story out, but apparently after the auditions, Ms. Crabapple and the seniors sat down to discuss all the candidates. When they got to my name, Ms. Crabapple said, "Terra's voice is great, but she doesn't quite *fit in*." Realizing I was being cut for my size, not my singing ability, Ashley and Sarah tried to reason with her, but she wouldn't budge. In the end, Ashley told her, "If you're going to cut Terra, then I don't want to be in this group," and she walked out.

I was shattered. It was devastating enough that this had been my last chance to make the team, but to find out that it was my size and not my voice that had kept me off the team all along felt so unfair. For weeks leading up to the auditions my mom would rehearse with me and give me notes on my pitch or enunciation. I remember going home that night and feeling like there was no way I could tell her why I had been cut. We never talked about me being little, and this would have forced me into a conversation I wasn't ready to have. I also felt like I couldn't betray Ashley's trust. She had already done so much for me and I didn't want our friendship to be tarnished by exposing that she had told me had happened during the audition.

Two days later, even though I knew I hadn't made the cut, I went to check out the list of names that Ms. Crabapple had posted on a bulletin board in the choir room. I was surprised when I saw Ashley's name, but my jaw dropped when I saw *my* name right under hers. Ashley later told me that the night after the audition Ms. Crabapple had called her to try to get her to change her mind about quitting. When she couldn't, she must have decided to back down and she put me on the team. As excited as I was finally to be in Premier, I was angry and hurt that Ms. Crabapple had dismissed me because of my size. It lit a fire under me to work harder than ever before. My mission in life became to prove to Ms. Crabapple that she was wrong about me. Going into senior year, I was all about Premier and making it the best choir season ever; by the end of that season we had placed first at the regional and national levels.

At the end of every season there was a show choir cabaret performance, and singers had to audition for solos and duets. Ashley and I auditioned for a duet where we used sign language, and I auditioned for a solo part singing "I Cain't Say No" from *Oklahoma*. Our duet didn't get picked, but I got my solo. That was the first time I had ever been picked to sing a solo during cabaret, and I was determined to show everyone that big things come in small packages. At that point in my life I wasn't confident as a solo performer and I remember standing backstage feeling anxious and shaky. Whenever I get nervous, my hands get cold, and when I walked out on that stage my hands were like ice. (To this day that's how I know I'm ready to perform; if my hands are warm I'm in trouble because it means I'm not pumped.) The only row I could see was the front row; the rest of the auditorium was total darkness. I knew my family and all my friends were out there somewhere, even Sam and his brother had come to the performance, but I decided to stare into the black abyss so I would feel like I was singing alone in my room.

The first twenty seconds were rough. Then it got awesome. When I perform, whether I do well or not, there's a crazy adrenaline rush that comes over me that is unlike anything else. It feels like all eyes are on me and I have control of everyone in the room. It's scary and exhilarating at the same time. I didn't know where Alee and Crystal were sitting, but by time my song was over I knew exactly where they were because they were cheering louder than everyone else in the room. After the show, students and teachers kept coming up to me and asking, "How did that big voice come out of that little body?" I loved the compliments and the attention; it was so inspiring to feel like I had an impact on the people around me and that I had changed their attitudes

Ashley and I getting ready for the end-of-year cabaret.

Onstage at the 1998 LPA conference in LA, performing my "I Cain't Say No" solo in the talent show.

about what little people can do. That was the moment I realized that *this* was what I wanted to do with my life.

But the sweetest moment of all was when Ms. Crabapple gave me a handwritten note from the orchestra teacher, telling me how proud she was of me. This was a woman Ms. Crabapple deeply respected, and I have always suspected that she read the note before passing it on to me because after that she treated me differently; she would talk to me about music and include me in conversations in class. Although we never spoke about what had happened, and she never gave me praise of any kind, I felt the shift in our dynamic was her way of acknowledging that she had underestimated me. It felt like my finish line.

||||||||||||||||||||

SENIOR YEAR ENDED ON A high, but what happened the following summer had me crashing back down to earth. Graduation happened to fall on the same day as my birthday, so my mom let me have a bunch of friends over for an unofficial graduation/birthday bash. Alee and Crystal were there with their boyfriends, Ashley and Sarah came with some choir kids, and then there were Sam and a few friends from work. It was the first time I had all my friend groups mixing together, so it was already a weird night integrating these very different worlds.

The party went late, so my mom let some of the stragglers stay the night. Long after everyone else had either crashed or gone home, Sam and I stayed up talking. I remember we were lying on the floor and I was leaning against this blue beanbag chair that made the most obnoxious sound any time you moved the slightest bit. Out of the blue Sam leaned over and kissed me. The kiss was nice, but at the same time I was freaked out. Sam was my best friend and I didn't want to lose what we had, but

On our way to prom! (From left to right: Crystal, Alee, me.)

once we kissed there was no way we could keep ignoring that deep down we wanted more than friendship of each other. After that, I would sneak out in the middle of the night and go to his house. Though we never had sex, we were very intimate—I was his first of many things, and he was my first for a few as well.

There was nothing weird between us until the night we kissed, and then Sam totally changed. The truth is, once we kissed he could never quite make the leap to the two of us going out on our own together in public. It was one thing when we were alone, but he would only go out on "dates" with me if we were part of a group. Even though he was the one who had initiated the kiss and had talked me into giving the relationship a try, he just couldn't get over his hang-ups about his girlfriend being a little person. He insisted he wanted us to be together, but then he would backpedal and say things like, "I feel like I'd be holding my daughter's hand instead of my girlfriend's," which made me feel insecure, like he didn't think I was good enough. I couldn't understand how he could love me and yet not want to be seen in public with me because of what other people thought, but I put up with it because there was a part of me that was just happy to have a boyfriend. Alee and Crystal had boyfriends all through high school and this was the first time that I didn't feel left out.

It was painful knowing that it was my size—something that was beyond my control—that was the only thing standing in the way of our relationship. As the summer wore on, I got more and more depressed. When I couldn't take it anymore, I told him we had to break up. Afterwards, I remember crying on the bathroom floor because I was so heartbroken. I felt so desperate; I even asked my mom about limb lengthening surgery. Thankfully, she put her foot down and wouldn't support me getting this painful procedure for the sake of a boy.

"He isn't worth the effort you're giving him if he can't accept who you are," she told me. "You have to love *yourself* first."

While I totally understand now what she was trying to tell me, at eighteen I was blinded by love and I would have done anything to make the pain of that heartbreak go away. All I wanted was for the boy I loved to go on a date with me and not be embarrassed.

A few days later, Sam called and begged to get back together with me. This time, he said, he would take me on a real date. Just the two of us. I was beyond excited. Picture this: An afternoon matinee of *Psycho* (not the Hitchcock classic, but the Gus van Sant remake with Vince Vaughn), in a tiny theater, during

33

the middle of the week. We were the only people in the entire theater except for one other couple. It was the worst experience ever. He was too embarrassed even to hold my hand in front of this roaring crowd of two moviegoers. That's when knew—if I had any respect for myself—I had to walk away. It took me a solid year to regain my confidence.

I wrote my first love song from heartbreak:

You're the last voice I hear every night
You're the one that I want, to hold me tight
You're the One I want
You're the one I need
Please tell me I'm the one you want,
and I'm the one you need.

You make me laugh
You make me cry
You bring a light into my life
You've always been there
Through weak and strong
Here with You is where I belong

You're the one I want
You're the one I need
Please tell me I'm the one You want,
and I'm the one you need.

But if it feels wrong
What more can I do
Oh, one more thing
I still love you
I still feel you
dreaming about you
if you only knew

What you would have
or What I would give
How I would treat you
for as long as we live

You're the one I want
You're the One I need
Please tell me I'm the one you want
and I'm the one you need.

I look back at these lyrics now and all I can see is a lovesick girl obsessed with an immature boy who couldn't accept her for who she was.

||||||||||||||||||||

AS AN ADULT, I DATED both average-height guys and LPs. In my twenties, I dated an average-sized guy whose twin was an LP. It was nice because he had a level of comfort with little people, but he wanted to be married with children, and I was not about that baby momma life at that point. The other average-sized guy I dated in my mid-twenties was less comfortable with little people. The hardest part about dating him was that he would allow himself to be triggered when we were out in public and people stared us. He would walk right up to people and get very confrontational. I think he felt like he was defending me, but it was way more mortifying for me than just to have people stare.

In general, I think people are curious about the unknown. With average-height guys, if they've never been with an LP before, there are always anatomy-related questions—basically, "will it fit?" Once a girlfriend gets to know you well enough, inevitably she will ask about the sex, "How does it work?" or "Does it feel different?" For the record: I've been with tall men who are not well endowed and LPs who are hung like donkeys—average size or LP, the anatomy is the same.

For the most part my serious, long-term relationships have been with LPs. Maybe it's because of the comfort level; if you're uncomfortable with me being little, it's hard for me to date you. With my husband, Joe Gnoffo (who has psedoachondroplasia, a form of short-limb dwarfism that is similar to achondroplasia but without our characteristic facial features), I honestly feel I would be with him no matter what; the connection we have goes beyond our size.

CHAPTER THREE

SPECTACULAR

After graduating high school what I really wanted was to audition for Radio City Music Hall's *Christmas Spectacular*. When I was growing up, every year at the national LPA conference, Radio City Music Hall would hold open auditions for the New York stage as well as for their traveling road companies. During the conference, there's an expo on the convention floor where booths are set up to sell everything from peddle extensions for driving, to special chairs and custom bikes. About ten years ago, LPA stopped hosting Radio City at conferences, but when I was growing up they would have a booth set up at the expo, where you could speak to a representative from Radio City if you were interested in auditioning. There would be a table stacked with fliers and a video monitor playing a loop of clips from the show so you could get an idea of the roles they were seeking to fill.

The three roles that they typically had for little people were the baby bear in the Nutcracker scene, a snowman who comes to life in the winter scene, and, of course, the elves in Santa's workshop. Usually the shorter LPs would get the baby bear and snowman, and if you were on the taller side you would only play the elf roles. Though it varied from city to city, they would typically hire five little people with one "swing" for each show. The "swing" is the understudy, so you had to know all the blocking for every role and be ready to jump in a half hour before show time if needed.

I never felt exploited by Radio City. In fact, back then LPs were given principal contracts, which meant we were paid more than most of the average-sized dancers and singers in the show (even though we were only on stage for a few minutes at a time). Whether you want to be a performer or not, Radio City is an appealing opportunity for little people. The pay is great—you go from working minimum wage at your local grocery store to pulling in over a grand a week for seasonal work—but the best thing about a Radio City gig (and probably the only reason that my mother agreed to let me do it in the first place) is that it comes with full medical benefits for the entire year. Before the Affordable Care Act, if you didn't have a job that offered medical benefits, people with dwarfism couldn't get insurance because it's considered a "preexisting condition." This was a big reason I kept going back to Radio City even after I didn't really need it for my career.

From the moment I found out about the auditions I couldn't wait until I was old enough to try out, but my mom was dead set against it: "Go to college, get a degree, and *then* you can do what you want." She wanted me to have the security that comes from an education and a steady job. I spent a year studying music education at a community college in San Antonio, but I was bored out of my mind. I was eighteen and I wanted to be a singer. My attitude then was that I was wasting my time learning about music theory and some old dead guys who wrote music hundreds of years before I was even born. So at the end of that school year, I convinced my mom to let me audition for Radio City and to take the fall semester off if I was cast. She wasn't crazy about the idea, but I guess she was hoping that the experience would satisfy my itch and that afterwards I would settle down and commit to staying in school.

At the audition, the first thing they had us do was march around the room. They wanted to see if, at minimum, we *could* march because little people struggle with timing. It was hilarious watching forty LPs marching around with right arms and legs together then left arms and legs together, like dyslexic robots. Most of the people auditioning were not dancers, so they didn't know how to walk on count much less march to a beat—which is ironic considering one of the most iconic scenes in the *Christmas Spectacular* is the "Parade of the Wooden Soldiers." Considering the precision of The Rockettes, Radio City was much more lenient with little people in terms of dance technique.

When Radio City called to tell me I had been cast as a principal in the road company and they were sending me to Branson, Missouri, from October to January, I was out of my mind with excitement. This was my first entertainment gig ever and they were paying me $1,200 a week for three months, which was an enormous amount of money for a 19-year-old. When they told me Branson, I said, "Awesome. I'm there." When I hung up the phone the first thing I did was pull out a map because I was like, "Where the hell is Branson?"

It was called a principal part, but, essentially, I was a baby bear, a snowman, and a (transgender) elf. I knew it wasn't a solo opportunity and that I wasn't exactly living my dream, but I felt like I was on a track, and that it was a good way to get my jitters out to see if I liked performing at this level. The experience opened my eyes to the world on so many levels. Most of the male performers in the cast were gay and, at that point in my life, it was such an eye opener because I had never met anyone who was openly gay before. I loved being a part of such an open and welcoming community, where everyone was allowed to be who they are and not feel judged or cast aside.

There were five other little people cast in the show and they came from all walks of life: there was an engaged Mormon couple, an alcoholic, a single mother of two, and then there was Charlie. How do I describe Charlie? In the three months that we were in Branson, he managed to have his car repossessed, all his possessions stolen, *and* he was chased by a pimp. Charlie had pituitary dwarfism, which is the result of a growth hormone deficiency. Pituitaries have bodies that are proportionate and they tend to have minimal health issues; they're just extremely short. Many of the munchkins in the *Wizard of Oz* had pituitary dwarfism.

Charlie was crazy and outgoing; you had no choice but to like him because he'd befriend you before you even had a chance to make up your mind about him. We spent the first two weeks rehearsing in Springfield, and the night before we were leaving for Branson, Charlie hooked up with a woman he'd met online. Late that night he came knocking on all our doors, asking if he could stay in one of our rooms because the woman he'd hooked up with was still in his room, and he was hiding from her until she left. I'm not sure where he ended up sleeping, but in the morning he told us, "You're never going to believe what happened. When I got back to my room everything was gone. She took *everything* in the room, including the mattress and the TV!"

Branson, Missouri, was like a run-down Vegas. They would bring in busses full of old white people; you'd look out into the audience and it would be a sea of white faces and purple-tinted hair. We did two shows a day during the week and three on Saturdays and Sundays with no days off, so after three months your body was shot. I had to glue my elf beard on for every single performance, so by January my face was so raw it was starting to look like I actually had a beard. But, I loved every moment of it. When the season ended, I went back to school for the spring semester, but I couldn't get performing out of my head. I auditioned for Radio City again in July and, when I got the call that they wanted me as a swing in Detroit the following Christmas, that was it for me and school.

||||||||||||||||||||

DETROIT IS WHERE I MET Tonya, who became one of my dearest friends as well as castmate on *Little Women: LA*. Radio City had put us up in an apartment complex about a half-hour drive from the venue, and Tonya was my roommate. Our room was a fully furnished double suite with a master bedroom that had a private bathroom with a shower and a smaller bedroom that only had access to a shared bathroom in the hallway with no shower and a tub. I still remember our very first day in Detroit. I had arrived before Tonya and I really wanted the room with the private shower, but I knew she was older and had been doing Radio City for years, so out of respect I decided to leave my luggage outside the room and let Tonya have first pick. She thought that was the nicest gesture and it worked out perfectly because she never takes showers and decided to take the room that only had the bathtub anyway.

Although I definitely felt nervous about what it would be like to live with a stranger for three months, once I met the sassy firecracker that is Tonya Renee Banks, I knew instantly we were going to hit it off. The first time she called me a "cow" I cried because I thought she was saying I was fat, but she was like, "*Girl*, that means I like you." Tonya turned out to be the best roommate I could have hoped for. I was twenty and she was in her 30s, so I really felt like she took me under her wing. She actually bought me my first cocktail at a bar; I'd only had wine coolers up to then, so I felt very grown up drinking my Amaretto Sour. The only thing we ever fought about was the thermostat, which she insisted on keeping at 80 degrees. Our room was like a tropical rainforest. Meanwhile, it was Michigan in the middle of a snowstorm and I'd be sweating with the window open. Tonya has not aged a day since I met her, and if you ask her how she stays looking so young she will tell you, "I don't smoke and black don't crack."

One morning, about a month in, we got a call ninety minutes before show time from the LP castmate who was our ride to the venue; his car was snowed in and he needed help digging it out. Tonya and I were freaking out because if you're not at the theater thirty minutes before show time, you don't perform. If that wasn't stressful enough, I was the swing so if *I* wasn't there, we were really in trouble. The apartment complex was a large circular building that was built around a pond. Our ride lived all the way on the other side of that pond, so it was either trudge a half-mile around on the ring road or cut through the middle, which was maybe twenty yards across. It had been snowing like crazy, and at this point the snow was so deep we couldn't even see the pond anymore, but I figured our best shot

for making it to the venue in time was to take our chances and cut through the middle. How deep could it be?

"How in the *hell* are we going to get across there?" Tonya asked, clearly skeptical and agitated by the whole situation.

"It's probably not that deep, and it will be faster than if we took the road," I reasoned.

Now, it should be stated for the record that Tonya is a woman from Southern California who hates the snow, and from the get-go she was not feeling my plan at all. When we first set out the snow was about knee-deep, but as we kept walking it was gradually getting deeper and deeper. I kept shouting to Tonya, who was behind me, "Stay to the right; we don't want to fall in the pond." The whole time, I could hear her voice behind me: "Oh, no...Oh, *hell no!*" By that point, the snow was up to our waists and Tonya was so pissed off she had picked up speed.

"You got me *fucked up*," I heard her say, gaining on me.

"Stop making me laugh, girl," I said. By that point I was laughing so hard I had to crouch down and cross my legs because I was dangerously close to peeing my pants.

"*Girl*, this is some bullshit," she said right as she was passing me. "This is some *bull...shit!*"

We kept moving forward and the snow just kept getting deeper and deeper. Then, when she was maybe ten feet ahead of me, I heard Tonya shout, "Terra, remind me to kick your ass when we get out of here."

That was it. I lost it and I couldn't stop laughing. I felt myself peeing, but it was one of those moments where once you start you can't stop. For a second it felt so warm and then almost instantly the urine froze my pants to the sides of my legs. When we finally made it across to our ride's apartment, we walked along the side of his patio around to where his car was parked. Not only had he been trying to shovel his car out with a broom, as soon as we rounded the corner we saw him pouring hot water over both of his tires. Simultaneously, Tonya and I shouted, "Noooo!!" But it was too late; his tires froze instantly. We ended up catching a ride with some of the dancers, but from that moment on I knew I loved Tonya, partly because she's bitter but mostly because a friend who can make you pee your pants with laughter, while trudging through waist-deep snow, is a friend for life.

||||||||||||||||||||

DETROIT IS ALSO WHERE I met Joe for the first time. He was doing Radio City in Chicago, but he had driven to Detroit to visit his best friend, who was in our cast. At the time, LPs in the touring companies were known for throwing big bashes at the beginning of every season, and that year's party definitely

lived up to its clever and subtle name: Drunkfest 2000. There were literally hundreds of Jell-O shots in the refrigerator of the apartment where they were having the party. I just remember staring at Joe like a crazy person the whole night. I didn't know too much about him, other than he had had grown up with average-sized parents and siblings and was half Polish/half Italian, but I just felt this instant attraction. When we were talking, I would laugh so hard that I didn't know how to control myself. I loved that I couldn't stop laughing around him and I kept wondering, *is it because I'm so attracted to this guy or is he really this funny?* Tonya remembers that when she first laid eyes on Joe, she asked me, "Who's that guy?" and I answered, "That's the man I'm going to marry."

The timing wasn't perfect (he was already in a relationship and I was dating a douchebag), but I was totally crushing on Joe and, as it turned out, he was crushing on me too. Towards the end of the party I was pretty hammered, so Joe offered to drive me back to my place. I wish I could look back on our first kiss as this soft, romantic moment, but I pretty much attacked Joe; it was a very lust- and alcohol-induced moment. Afterward, I felt very confused. On the one hand I was wracked with guilt because we were both dating other people, but at the same time I felt something different with Joe than I had ever experienced before. It felt like I had found my soul mate.

The very next day his friend came up to me and said, "Hey, I heard about you and Joe hooking up last night." He knew every detail about what had happened, which was both humiliating and hurtful. I thought Joe and I had shared this deep connection, but it turned out I had just spent the night with a player and I had fallen for his game. After that, I wanted nothing to do with Joe Gnoffo. I didn't speak to him for years.

CHAPTER FOUR

EVIL ELF

After Detroit, I decided not to go back to school. I don't have many regrets in life, but I do regret not having a college education. I hate not finishing something I've started, but I wanted to make a career as a singer. At that time I felt if I don't do something *right now*, it's never going to happen. I had this intense drive to succeed, and I wanted to start performing right away. It was one of those moments where I felt, *If I believe in myself* (which I did) *and I take that leap of faith* (which I did), *it will lead me to my dream* (which it did...eventually).

So, in August of 2001, I loaded as many of my possessions as I could fit into my little Honda, took the $200 I still had in my savings from Radio City, and drove 1,200 miles along Interstate 10, all the way from San Antonio to California. Right before I moved I had come across a post through the LPA listserv that MTV was casting the third season of their docu-series *True Life*. They were looking for little people with unusual jobs, or who were considering limb-lengthening surgery, or who worked in the entertainment industry. I contacted the producer and told her that I was moving out to Los Angeles to pursue my dream of becoming a singer. She must have liked my story because right away she wanted to send a film crew out to San Antonio to film my journey. They followed me out to LA, where they filmed my early struggles to find work; to this day, people still recognize me from that episode.

In Los Angeles, I moved in with my old friend Amy Morris. We'd met at my first LPA conference and have been close since the age of fourteen. We're the same age, we're both blondes, and we're both achon, so a lot of the time our neighbors couldn't tell us apart and they'd be like, "Hey, Amy," when I walked by or vice versa. Amy had moved to Los Angeles from Michigan and almost immediately, she started working at Starbucks and got onto a management track. Even though she had initially moved to LA because of the performance opportunities, she ended up staying because of the little people scene.

Me and my roomie, Amy Morris.

Two months after I moved to LA, Tonya and I both auditioned as dancers for the teaser to *Austin Powers in Goldmember*. Out of the three hundred little people who auditioned, they picked ten of us to be principals. This was the first job I ever got where I was actually hired as a dancer—no elf beards or bear costumes—and that was the most empowering feeling I had ever had as a performer. We spent one week rehearsing the choreography and one week filming the teaser, which was a re-creation (using all little people) of the opening musical number from the first *Austin Powers* film. They had hired over a hundred LP extras and to this day I've never seen so many little people working on set at one time. I wouldn't be surprised if the last time that happened was for *The Wizard of Oz*. Joe was actually an extra in the marching band, but I was still pissed at him from our night in Detroit so I totally gave him the cold shoulder.

They put Tonya and I in the front row, splitting Verne Troyer, with the other principal dancers and a full LP marching band behind us (and again it was right-leg-right-hand, left-leg-left-hand; during rehearsals they looked like the most uncoordinated marching band ever). Verne is a huge inspiration for little people in the entertainment industry, so it was mind-blowing to be working with him on my first real job after arriving in LA. I just remember thinking: they chose *me*. I felt like a superstar, like I had made it. I even had my own trailer. That was it. I was hooked. I was only in the teaser for the movie, but I was making almost a thousand dollars a day doing something that I loved. It was such a rush. I felt like nothing could stop me. There was no way I could go back to San Antonio now.

Little did I know that it would be a while before I would have that feeling again. While I may have been ready to take on Hollywood, I quickly learned that Hollywood wasn't necessarily ready for me. Turns out that there's not a lot of mainstream work in Hollywood for four-foot-two blondes with dwarfism, no matter how talented you are. Funnily enough, I'm actually too tall for a little person in the entertainment industry. I was always so proud of my two inches, but ironically, when I got to Los Angeles, I learned that casting calls for little people are always capped at four feet. I ended up having to list myself as 4' 0" on IMBD so I wouldn't keep getting shut out of auditions.

Los Angeles has the biggest community of little people in the country. You get a lot of characters out here, not just musicians, artists, and performers, but all kinds who can't get regular jobs because they're so offbeat. There's a lot of entertainment work out there for LPs, but most of the time they're just looking for someone to fill a costume so you don't necessarily need to have any talent. You'll go to auditions and they'll ask, *how do you feel about wrestling in a bunny costume?* Or, *how do you feel about wearing a sombrero and having people eat chips and salsa out of it?*

Basically, if you're a little person, the work in Hollywood is seasonal. If it's October you know you're going to be auditioning for the role of an elf; November, it's Cupids; January is leprechaun season; and so on. So, while it's not hard for a little person to find work in the industry, if your dream is to have a legit career as a singer or dancer (like mine had been for as far back as I can remember) those opportunities are a lot harder to come by.

|||||||||||||||||||||

THAT FALL RADIO CITY WANTED to send me back to Detroit, but at that point I felt like I needed to move forward; if they weren't sending me to New York, I needed to look for a better opportunity. Meanwhile, a friend had hooked me up with an audition for Ozzie Osbourne's Merry Mayhem Tour, which was to kick off Halloween night in Tucson, Arizona. It was slightly less money than Radio City would have been, but it was a longer gig so I reasoned that in the end I would make more money and it would be better for my career.

I was hired to play an "Evil Elf" and we were being paid to hype up the crowd—or so I thought. There were six little people on the tour, four men and two women, and we shared a tour bus. The minute we got on the bus I called dibs on the bottom bunk. I love the bottom bunk because you get to fall asleep to the sound of the engine running and the wheels rolling; to me it's like one of those white noise machines that soothe you to sleep. Every bunk had a TV and a curtain so you could close yourself off from the world, or at least have a little bit of privacy from the rest of the bus. The mini kitchen was always stocked with beer, snacks, soft drinks, food, and more food. Everything you could ask for. It felt like such a VIP experience.

Our "training" was more like an orientation: they told us what they expected from us on the tour bus and did a fitting for our costumes. Everyone was warm and welcoming. They were like, "The crew is a family; everyone sticks together." We were told our job was to "mess with the crowd," which right away should have been a red flag because messing with an Ozzy Osbourne and Rob Zombie crowd is probably not the sanest idea in the world. We had to wear these itchy, black synthetic wigs, steampunk top hats, contacts that turned our eyes white, and a full face of makeup that made us look like the unholy children of Kiss and Insane Clown Posse. Our costumes were basically black onesies with handmade light-up skeletons glued to the front and 3-pound battery packs strapped to our backs. By the end of the night, the skeletons would be so hot that the glue would melt, and we'd have to resort to pinning them on—one of them even started smoking and caught fire the first night while one of us was wearing it. They had these two Power Wheels, which are basically battery-powered vehicles for children, that they had customized with spikes and silver and black paint—for all I know, underneath they were pink Barbie Jeeps.

On opening night, I remember we were told by our tour wrangler to take our Evil Power Wheels and run into people in the mosh pit, spill their drinks, and get them really pissed off. I thought they were kidding at first, but they had set up this little studio area backstage with shelves of "props" (mostly plastic skeletons and morbid-looking baby dolls with bloody knives sticking out of their necks), for us to smack people with as we ran them over. It was the worst idea I had ever heard. (I don't know about you, but I'm 4 foot 2 inches and I can *still* run faster than a Power Wheel.) When I voiced my concerns about the possibility of people getting violent, the response was basically: *Don't worry, we put riding lawn mower engines in your Power Wheels so they'll move much faster*. As optimistic and stupid as I was at twenty-one, I thought, *Perfect! What can go wrong?*

The doors opened and, as the throngs of metalheads began filing into the venue, the scene defined mayhem. You could get high just by being in the same building as these fans. Most were dressed in black jeans and either Ozzy, Rob Zombie, or Mudvayne T-shirts. The opening band was about to hit the stage and the mosh pit was full, so it was show time for the Evil Elves. I hopped into one of the souped-up Evil Power Wheels with my partner and we were the first two out in the crowd. He was shaking his doll around with one arm and steering with the other as we drove into hell. Let me explain something to you: we may look small, but even though we are "little" people, we have similar size-weight proportions as average-sized people. That car had to be at least 300 pounds, add to that the weight of two adult Evil Elves, and you've got a slow-moving but highly effective battering ram. Now, try to picture bumping this battering ram into somebody who is mentally off.

I'll never forget the look on the face of the first guy we rammed into as he looked down at the puddle that was once his $8 solo cup of beer and then back up at the two (now-petrified) Evil Elves who had caused him to spill it. His expression went from *what-the-fuck?* to *I'm-going-to-kill-you* in about two seconds flat. He looked like he wanted to rip my head off and spit down my neck.

"We gotta get out of here," I shouted.

The reverse on our Evil Power Wheel was so slow that we had no choice but to keep going straight, so my partner stepped on the gas and we lurched forward at medium speed. As we drove through the pit, knocking into increasingly angry fans left and right to escape the first guy, we began to collect a gang of rabid metalheads behind us, who by now were pissed off enough to shout: "Kill those fucking midgets!"

As sweat, makeup, and beer ran down my face and into my already blurry contact-covered eyes, I heard my partner scream, "My makeup. I can't see!" We were both in hell and all we wanted was to be out of the pit. Through one clenched and stinging eye, I could just make out an exit sign about five yards ahead.

"To the right! Go! Go! Go! Exit ahead!" I shouted.

Then, all of a sudden, this huge, burly biker dude caught up to us, plucked my partner out of the driver seat and carried him back off into the pit, as his screams of "Nooo! Nooo! Nooo!" were swallowed up by the crowd. For a split-second I thought about being a hero, but I was worried for my own safety and it was every Evil Elf for herself. I grabbed the steering wheel, slid my left foot over to gas pedal, and floored it to the exit sign. When I got to the door, frantically waving my all-access wristband, the security guard posted there asked me if I needed help. (*Really? What part of me shouting, "HELP, HELP, PLEASE HELP!" over and over while fleeing an angry mob gave you that impression?*) I attempted to explain, more calmly this time, "They just took my friend. You gotta help him." As security ran into the pit to save my partner, I hopped back onto my Evil Power Wheel and drove it straight into the nearest ladies' room.

I'm not gonna lie—I hid in the bathroom for the next three hours and didn't come out until the show was over. I was so beside myself with fear, I didn't know what else to do. This was not what I had signed up for. People kept stopping in the bathroom and taking photos in the Evil Power Wheel, while I washed the sweat, beer, and makeup off my face in a public sink. I was like: *Be my guest. Take as many photos as you want. You can take the damn car for all I care.* I was dumb enough to do what they had asked, and I ended up putting myself into a situation that was not only degrading but that had put my life in danger.

At the end of the night, I finally plucked up the courage to venture from the sanctuary of the restroom just as another Evil Elf was exiting the men's room next door; he still had on a full face of sweat- and beer-streaked makeup and looked like he had been through the ringer. Turned out the restrooms were a Safe Zone that night because after he was messed with he had decided to call the bathroom home for the evening as well. Back on the tour bus we regrouped with the rest of the Evil Elves. My partner, who had been dragged into the mosh pit, had been rescued by security. Thankfully, other than looking roughed

up and having a bloody lip he was largely intact. The six of us swapped horror stories and agreed things had to change or we would quit. When Sharon Osbourne got wind of what had happened and that we were all ready to leave the tour, she called a meeting on our bus with the tour wrangler and a few other head honchos. Appalled by what had happened, the higher-ups apologized. Apparently, they had never done anything like that on tour before and what had seemed to somebody from production like a good idea at the time had turned into a total disaster. No shit.

By the next city, everything changed. Our instructions now were to ride around (with security) and *only* hype the crowd; no need to run people over or spill their beers anymore. As added incentive for us to stay, they also arranged for us to take pictures with fans for local charities. We were a few weeks away from Christmas, so they put out the word that if you brought a toy to donate you would get a free photo Ozzy's Evil Elves. If you didn't bring a toy, you could buy a photo and the money would go to a local children's charity in whatever city we were in.

Just like that, our experience went from "fuck this" to "I love this job" and it turned into something that I was actually proud to be a part of.

The tour was supposed to run through the end of the year, but unfortunately Ozzy fractured his leg in the shower. After two weeks in ten cities the tour was canceled. I couldn't believe I had given up Radio City for a two-week job. What was I going to do now?

CHAPTER FIVE

FAYGO

When the Merry Mayhem Tour ended, Amy and I moved into a two-bedroom apartment in North Hollywood. I floated around for a while, bouncing from job to job doing temp work, most of it was sales but I never felt like I was a good salesperson. I hated cold calling; a lot of the time it just felt like a scam, but I did it because it was a paycheck. I needed a consistent income to pay rent, so after about a year I took a full-time job as a medical underwriter for a brokerage company that represented big insurance carriers.

My job was to go through people's medical records and evaluate their eligibility for health insurance. I loved the people I worked with, but I hated the job because it was so depressing. Initially we would decline people through the mail, but then some of them would call wanting to state their case. These conversations were always so heartbreaking because often they had been turned down for something as simple as asthma, or if they had been on anxiety or depression medication within the last ten years. I remember there would be times I would get off a call and I'd be sobbing at my desk. I could relate to what the people calling were going through because if it wasn't for my job, I wouldn't have had health insurance either.

I didn't know how to handle it. I started to gain weight and I sank deeper and deeper into depression. On top of that, my agent would call weekly to send me out on auditions, but I'd have to pass because I couldn't get the time off work. He would give me guilt trips like, "What's the point of me signing you if you're not willing to go out on these auditions?" After I while, I was so embarrassed that I started to avoid his calls. The reason I stayed as long as I did was because I loved the people I worked with and I needed the income, but I was stuck in a rut. Every time I had to turn down an audition because of work it felt like a piece of my dream was dying, but I was my only source of income and in order to support myself I needed that job. It felt like a no-win situation.

I stayed way longer than I should have and then, just when I needed it, I came to a crossroads. After two years, my employer wanted me to get industry certification, which would have meant going back to school—and having even less time to go out on auditions. I knew being a medical underwriter wasn't what I wanted to do with the rest of my life and that I desperately I needed a change, so this ended up being the best thing that could have happened at that point in my life because it forced me to get out before it really was too late.

I knew that if I left my job and found some kind of consistent part-time work I would have less money, but I'd have a more flexible schedule so I could go on auditions. I didn't want to go back to temp work, so I asked myself: *Other than entertainment, what do I love? There were always dogs in our house growing up. I know a lot about dogs. What if I try grooming?* So I applied at groomers all around the Los Angeles area. The one that called me back was Petco, which also paid for my training. Groomers earned an hourly rate plus commission on every dog groomed—so we were always trying to upsell people on the services to make a higher commission. I truly loved grooming; the only problem was that I wasn't bringing in enough money to cover expenses both for my car and my apartment. I went from making a little under forty grand a year, which had allowed a pretty comfortable lifestyle for a 24-year-old, to a few hundred dollars a week. It was a drastic change. I couldn't afford to go out, buy clothes, or even grab a cup of coffee. For a while there, flip-flops were my jam because I couldn't afford a new pair of shoes. The one decent piece of furniture I had was an Ikea bed that I had purchased while I was still working as a medical underwriter, but I felt earning less money as a groomer was a sacrifice I needed to make.

Meanwhile, I had missed Radio City for the past two years. It wasn't my passion, but at least it was performing so not doing it felt like a void in my life. I was really soul-searching, so I thought: *I'll do Radio City to get health insurance for the year and then I'll come back to grooming. Maybe I'll open my own shop.* I was in a freefall, with my dream receding on the horizon, and I just wanted to ground myself with something I was passionate about. I talked my manager at Petco into giving me a three-month leave to do Radio City in Denver and then to transfer me to a location in San Antonio.

When I left Los Angeles to do Radio City in Denver, I walked away from my apartment, my roommate, my then-boyfriend—everything. It was a clean break, an end to one chapter of my life and (I hoped) a promising new beginning. I spent three months living in a hotel in Denver, working as a swing for Radio

City. It was a grueling experience, but I needed the money and the health insurance to cover me for the coming year. When the show ended, I moved back to San Antonio and started grooming for Petco again. The best thing about my mom is that, no matter what, she will always have an open door for her children. When I was home, I didn't have to pay rent so I could save what little I was earning, but she was also basically like, "*This* is why you need to go back to school." The *last* thing I wanted to hear was, "I told you so." My mom is very accepting, but she never understood the life I chose to live. By my age, she was already settled down and had a stable job. She felt like performing was no way to live your life.

Almost immediately I regretted my decision to leave Los Angeles because I felt like I was giving up on my dreams, and after a few months, I was losing my mind at home. I decided to reach out to my friend Joey Fatale, whom I had met in 1995 at the Denver LPA conference. For years, Joey had been trying to get me to join his little person Kiss tribute band called (what else?) Mini Kiss, but the timing was never right so I had always turned him down. Joey, aka Mini Gene Simmons, had a type of dwarfism called spondyloepiphyseal dysplasia (or SED for short), which typically results in features like average-sized head, hands, and arms, but a rather short torso, legs, and neck. He had been doing Mini Kiss for a decade, and back in the day, their act was basically four dudes dressed up as Kiss, standing on top of a bar, lip-syncing to a CD while air-playing inflatable toy guitars. The bars would hire them to be entertainment but it was more about the makeup and costumes than performing the songs. Once they transitioned to actually using live vocals with a backing track, Joey realized he needed a woman to sing because Paul Stanley's voice is so high. Enter: Mini Paulina Stanley.

The last I had heard from Joey was a year earlier when he asked me to join them on tour with A Perfect Circle, but I wasn't ready to leave my job so I had turned him down. When I finally broke down and reached out to Joey, within a week I was on a flight to LA to perform on an episode of *The George Lopez Show*. In real life George is a huge Kiss fan, so they came up with the idea to have Mini Kiss perform on an episode of the show called "George Buys a Vow." Since it was a SAG job, they flew me first class from San Antonio to Los Angeles to sing "Endless Love" with Mini Kiss during the vow renewal with George's wife on the show. Picture your first gig back in Hollywood after working as a dog groomer in San Antonio for six months; you're flying first class and meeting celebrities on set. I had that whole sense of "I've made it" all over again, and I didn't want the journey to end. It felt like I had come home. That's when I knew I wasn't going back to dog grooming. I was born to be a performer and I was going to keep working in the entertainment industry as long as there was work out there for me. I don't know if it was destiny or sheer force of will, but from that day on I never had to work a 9-to-5 job again.

After *The George Lopez Show*, once or twice a week on average I'd fly from San Antonio to a new city to perform with Mini Kiss as Mini Paulina Stanley. We were traveling so much that sometimes we would forget what city we were in and Joey would shout into the mic, "What's up, Baltimore?!"—only problem was, we were in Boston. It happened so often that we had to have a cheat sheet taped to the stage with the name of whatever city we were in so we could keep track of where we were. I was basically making in one night what I would have made working three weeks at Petco. We performed all over the world: Sweden, Mexico, Turkey, Canada, plus every major US city and some you never even knew existed. We played bars, festival, clubs, bar mitzvahs, Sweet Sixteens, frat houses—you name it. Prior to joining the band, I didn't know a single Kiss song. I was definitely more of a pop music fan and I just remember being incredibly nervous. All of a sudden I was singing and dancing to karaoke tracks of "I Was Made for Loving You," "Beth," "Rock and Roll All Nite," "Lick It Up," and "Calling Doctor Love," often in front of thousands of people. At the time iPods weren't really a thing, so we were totally dependent on a CD for the backup music. If the CD jumped it wasn't a big deal for the other members of the band who were air-playing their instruments, but it was a total nightmare for the singer (i.e., *me*) who was responsible for knowing where we were supposed to be in the song—we definitely had a few Milli Vanilli moments. I loved that I was able to sing for a living, but I was living my dream through someone else's songs. I wasn't as bothered that it wasn't my music I was performing, as much as I was that nobody knew who I was behind all the makeup. If I was getting applause it was as Mini Paulina, not as Terra Jolé. It was a blast traveling the world, but I wanted more.

|||||||||||||||||||||

WE PLAYED SOME OF THE most obnoxious venues you could ever imagine, but there were definitely a few experiences I will never, ever forget. I remember one time performing on a picnic table in the basement of a fraternity house. The ceiling was so low we couldn't jump or we'd hit our heads, but we had to be on the table because otherwise nobody could see us, the crowd was so dense. One of the most memorable experiences was a gig we were hired to perform for a radio station in Chicago on opening day at Wrigley Field.

We were scheduled to arrive at the venue around 6:00 am, so we had to be fully made up and ready to go at 5:00 am. When the car picked us up, all I could think about was how pissed off I was that we didn't have time to stop and get something to eat. All of a sudden, we heard a siren coming up behind us, and our driver pulled over to the side of the road. He rolled down the window and a cop looked into the back of the car. We were all holding our breath and looking at each other like, what is this cop going think when he sees all of us—Kiss makeup, wigs, costumes, and all—in the back of this Cadillac Escalade?

"Mini Kiss!" he said, all excited. "I heard on the radio you guys were in town. I'm a huge fan."

We were speechless. He asked us if we would take some photos with him and then gave us a police escort to the bar—and that wasn't even the weirdest thing that happened that day.

When we got to the bar, the place was hopping with Cubs fans. It was directly across the street from Wrigley Field, and every single person there was decked out from head to toe in Cubs gear. They had set up a stage that was twenty feet long and ten feet wide, with a felt top like a pool table—probably to soak up all the spilled beer. I was in awe how many people were already hammered at six o'clock in the morning. Mancow Muller, a Chicago-based shock jock whose show, *Mancow's Morning Madhouse*, rivaled Howard Stern in its outrageousness, took the stage.

"I've got a lot of tickets to give out," he said, pumping up the crowd. "You guys are going to be doing some crazy things today."

By the time we got backstage, there were already two huge blocks of ice on the stage and two people had been sitting on them bare-assed for fifteen minutes just to get tickets to opening day at Wrigley. But the big prize of the morning was a set of four box seat tickets.

"This is going to be the hardest challenge of the day," Man Cow shouted into the mic. "Are you ready?"

"Yeah, we're ready!" the crowd shouted back.

Turning to face us backstage, Man Cow unzipped his pants, peed into a water bottle, and then poured the still steaming liquid into a solo cup. "First person to drink this will get four box seat tickets." Immediately four arms shot up into the air. Mancow picked this dude from the crowd and he came up onstage, looking so excited and patting himself on the back that he was about to win his opening day tickets.

"You have to drink it down to the bottom," Mancow reminded him as he handed the guy the steaming cup of piss.

The guy put the cup to his mouth, closed his eyes, tipped back his head, and drank every last drop of Mancow's urine. Then he held up the cup up in the air and the entire audience erupted in cheers and applause.

"Are you guys ready for the performance?" Mancow asked the crowd.

Then all of a sudden, the guy threw up the urine back into the cup. Mancow grabbed the tickets out of the guy's hands and said, "New prize. Whoever drinks *this* gets the tickets." Then this woman hopped up onto the stage and took the cup from Mancow. She downed about half of it and started to gag.

"No, no," Mancow said into the mic. "You gotta keep it down."

At that point, I straight up was on the side of the stage dry heaving. After she had downed every last drop of the urine puke, Mancow handed the woman the tickets. The look on her face was so proud, like she was bringing home the bacon for her husband.

I don't recall a single thing about our performance that day. I just remember thinking the whole thing was so fucked up and twisted, and feeling relieved in the end we hadn't had time for breakfast.

llllllllllllllllllll

ONE OF THE CRAZIEST JOBS we ever did was an annual five-day music festival in southeastern Ohio called the Gathering of the Juggalos, where Insane Clown Posse was headlining. We were short a drummer, so I suggested Joe fill in as Mini Peter Criss. After years of giving him the cold shoulder every time we ran into each other on a job or at party, I had decided to reach out to Joe after I moved back to San Antonio. At the time, I felt lonely and isolated and I had this sudden need to reach out and feel connected to something that made me feel good.

When I decided to call him, I was sitting on the lawn outside the Big House. My mother was still saddled with the two properties then and had to rent them to keep up with the payments. She couldn't afford a landscaper, so she had to do all the mowing and maintenance herself. Whenever I was home, I would help her out. I remember as the phone rang I had butterflies in my stomach, but once Joe answered and we started talking it was like no time had passed. We just picked up where we had left off.

We talked through what had happened between us in Detroit to the point where I was comfortable hanging out again, although I wasn't necessarily sure if I fully trusted him yet. If I'm being honest, though, I was still crushing on him hard, so the fact that Joe is an amazing drummer and made us look that much more like a "real" band was really just a good excuse to bring him on the road with us. The venue was in Nelson Ledges Quarry Park in Portage County, Ohio—basically, the middle of nowhere—and after this festival the place should have been

condemned. When we arrived, we were told that most of the festivalgoers had been camping there all week, and if the smell was anything to go on it could have been twice that long. There were no showers, few trees, and row after row of overflowing Porta Potties. Did I mention there were no showers? The stench that hung in the air was like rancid body odor mixed with Jolly Ranchers. There were swarms of bees everywhere you went; you could hear them buzzing all around you as you walked through the campground.

At first, we couldn't figure out what could make that smell. The unwashed festivalgoers were responsible for the body odor, but what could account for the fruity smell? Eventually we learned that it came from a regional fruit-flavored soft drink (similar to Fanta), called Faygo. It's referenced in several ICP songs and had been a staple at their concerts, the story goes, ever since Violent J threw an open bottle at a row of hecklers. At the time, I didn't know enough about Faygo or Insane Clown Posse to recognize the sickly-sweet smell, or to know what it forewarned we would be in for later that day.

While we could travel with guitars (to air-play), we couldn't always travel with a full drum kit, so for this particular venue we had rented another band's drums. Our "greenroom" was a shed like building behind the stage where we could get dressed and put on our Mini Kiss faces. We were each supposed to be responsible for our own makeup, but I usually just ended up doing most of the band's makeup myself. We used airbrush paint that wasn't really meant to go on a person's skin, but the pigment showed up beautifully, and when it dried it wasn't sticky. The only problem was it would run when it came in contact with sweat or—we would soon find out—liquid of any kind.

Backstage, just as we were about to go on, the stage manager came up to us and said, "Don't worry if they throw Faygo at you; that means they like you. If they start throwing turkey legs at you, whatever you're playing should be your last song. It means they hate you." The magician who had just left the stage said as he was passing us, "Don't worry. They only throw one or two bottles and you can see them coming to know when to duck."

We were like, "Wait...I'm sorry, *what?*" But, we didn't have much time to consider what was about to go down, because suddenly we were being called out onto this huge stage, with massive metal pillars and dozens of speakers taller than any member of our band. As soon as we walked out onto the stage, we were greeted by the roar of thousands of crazy ICP fans cheering us on.

"Let's do this," I shouted in the mic, so the sound guy would know to press play on the CD.

Our first song was "I Was Made for Loving You," and from the very first chord the crowd went nuts. All of the sudden we were in a war zone. You couldn't duck fast enough from one plastic bottle being thrown at you before three more were coming at you from all different directions. It was like every single person in the crowd simultaneously had the same idea: shake up a two-liter bottle of soda, slightly twist open the cap to where it's exploding like a sprinkler, and then throw it at the band member of your choice on the stage. Within minutes there were *hundreds* of exploding Faygo bottles strewn across the stage. I was getting hit with bottles so relentlessly that I couldn't even sing—not because I was in pain (which I was), but because I was laughing so hard at the ridiculousness of the situation. The fact that these fans were throwing Faygo at us meant they *liked* us; meanwhile, I was just doing my best not to get killed.

Then—*SMASH*—an exploding can of beer hit me in the eye. Faygo bottles were easier to avoid because they were so huge they were easy to spot as they came hurtling at you, but the beer seemed to have come out of nowhere. Instantly I could feel my right eye closing up as it began to swell. I remember telling the crowd, "That's gonna leave a mark." At this point I wasn't singing at all; I was just laughing and trying to survive. I watched as Joey stood at the front of the stage for one of his air solos, and a dude wearing a Super Soaker backpack filled with purple Faygo drenched him from head to toe. "Looks like they've got Grape over here," he laughed into the mic, just as I got drenched stage left with what tasted like Orange Faygo.

Crap, not only could I not see out of one eye from the beer can, but the Faygo had now liquefied my makeup and caused it to drip into my one good eye. Now I couldn't see anything. I heard Joe in the back, playing drums and screaming, "I'm a fucking sitting duck back here." Meanwhile, I could hear the *clank, clank, clank* as his drums were pelted with bottles of Faygo. It was target practice. I could see the guy who owned the drums on the side of the stage, screaming, "Noooo! Oh, noooo!!!" as he helplessly watched his drum set getting beat down by Faygo.

Joey stopped air-playing and, with the chords for "Rock and Roll All Nite" still playing in the background, took off his bass, and started knocking the bottles away with it as they flew towards Joe like he was in a batting cage.

"T, get behind me," he shouted, and then to the sound guy, "Last song."

That was our finale. We were supposed to be on stage for an hour, but we cut it down to a ten-minute set due to our infamous beat down by Faygo. Coming off the stage we looked like we had been through the ringer. My eye was swelling and bees were swarming. All I wanted was a shower and to *never, ever* perform at any ICP event again.

Later, Joe told me that during the first song he got hit in the mouth by a two-liter bottle and had to leave the stage for a second because he couldn't tell if he was bleeding or if it was his lipstick. When he told me that I was dying with laughter. Why he came back on the stage for more punishment, I will never understand. I'm not exaggerating when I say that after our set you could not see the stage floor. There were so many bottles of Faygo and so much shit all over the stage that it took dozens of stagehands an entire hour to clean it. After that job, I never looked at a bottle of Faygo the same way again.

My mom was not excited about me doing Mini Kiss at all. She didn't understand my lifestyle of working till one o'clock in the morning, surrounded by alcohol. When I came home from the ICP show with a black eye, she just shook her head and said, "You need to quit this job."

In the two years that I was with the band, Joey and I were the only consistent members; people cycled through faster than running water—the only requirements were that you had to be short and slightly stupid to take this job.

In 2007, Universal Records gave us the opportunity to release a single for "I Was Made for Loving You" with the Berman Brothers, the Grammy-winning producers of "Who Let the Dogs Out." We recorded the track in New York and released it under the band name Mini Rockerz. Then we flew to Sweden to film a music video with the Berman Brothers. I thought I was going to be set for life, but it didn't work out that way. They gave Joey 40 percent of the profits and out of that he offered me 5 percent, which I thought was totally unfair. I felt that my voice was the only live instrument on the track; I was the only one in the studio and I was doing all the work. We argued and he came up to 10 percent, but I still felt it wasn't a fair split. I wasn't being greedy. I was making less than him on the tours, and I was okay with that because Mini Kiss was *his* band—he dealt with all the bookings, contract issues, and scheduling—but I was determined to fight for equality on this track. After the single was released, and after two years of touring with Mini Kiss, I decided to leave the band because I felt like I couldn't do it anymore if wasn't being treated fairly.

Joey and I did not part on good terms, which I regret to this day. I remember arguing with him and telling I'm was going to do my own thing. I had come up with the idea to perform as a mini Britney Spears, and he swore up and down that it wasn't going to work. But he must have seen the potential because he went right out and bought the URL MiniBritney.com, which to this day redirects you to the Mini Kiss website. Four years later, Joey had a heart attack while on tour and passed away, so I was never able to reconcile with him. I wish I had the chance to tell him how grateful I was for my time in Mini Kiss and for all that I learned from him about the business. First and foremost, he taught me that even though we were a mini tribute band, the work didn't have to be demeaning or exploitative.

Mini Kiss wouldn't have taken off the way it did if it weren't for Verne Troyer and the *Austin Powers* movie series, because after Mini Me everybody wanted mini-entertainers. And, if it weren't for Joey and Mini Kiss, I never would have become a mini impersonator myself. Once I started performing as Mini Britney I realized that I could take control of my career. I am very grateful to Joey for that. He gave me an opportunity that changed my life.

CHAPTER SIX

LEAVING LAS VEGAS

After I left Mini Kiss, I knew I needed to find a way to move back to Los Angeles. Determined to prove Joey wrong, I went to a J.C. Penny Portrait Studio and took photos for a flier that I then plastered around every bar in San Antonio. I can still see the look of total confusion on the photographer's face when I showed up for my portrait session in a little schoolgirl outfit and pigtail braids tied up with pink feathers.

My $300 investment paid off because right away I was contacted by a guy in Austin who had come across one of my fliers and who wanted to hire Mini Britney to perform at his Super Bowl 2007 party. He was a young guy who must have been making decent money as a programmer because he had gone all out for his computer geek friends. In his backyard, he'd set up a buffet and a huge block of ice from which they were doing shots of tequila and vodka. The stage was a wooden table and he'd rented a little portable karaoke machine that had a microphone plugged into it. It was the cheesiest venue I ever

played, but I hopped up on that table in my schoolgirl outfit and sang my heart out to "Baby One More Time."

After this job, I contacted a booking agent and pretty quickly I was getting hired to perform at clubs and events all over the country. Since I had never done anything like this before, I based the contract I used as Mini Britney on the one Joey had used for Mini Kiss, which even had a clause in it that the venues hiring us couldn't use the word "midget" or any demeaning language to promote us. If they did, we would still be paid but would not have to perform. In May of 2007, I was hired to perform at a cabaret-style theater in New York City called The Box, which was famous for its eccentric performance art and was hot among celebrities and New York's underground club kid scene. This was my first legit gig as Mini Britney, but little did I know then that this one night would catapult my career as a mini performer into a whole new realm.

That night I witnessed the most dark and twisted variety show I had ever seen. There were all kinds of burlesque and avant-garde performers on the bill, and I was by far the tamest act of the night. There were drag queens, fire blowers, and fire-eaters. There was a woman who painted her vagina on stage and then sat on a canvas, which she then sold to people in the audience at the end of her performance (and, yes, I bought some of her "art"). There was another woman whose entire act consisted of simulating an abortion. I remember gagging backstage as she shoved a dull knife into her vagina and a softball-sized silicone ball and fake blood poured out onto the stage. There was also a drag queen who sat on a bottle of whiskey, walked around the stage with it hanging out of her butt, and then pulled it out and took a swig from it. And then, of course, there was me in my little Britney outfit.

Lindsay Lohan, who was at the peak of her tabloid popularity, happened to come to the club that night, and from the moment she walked in it was total mayhem. Paparazzi and hordes of publicity people seemed to appear out of thin air, and there were flashes going off everywhere. My greenroom happened to be next door to the headliner's, who was a close friend of Lindsay's. I remember, he would always stand in front of his mirror and prep his manhood so he had a huge package when he went out onstage. When Lindsay came backstage to hang with him that night, we chatted for a bit while she put her lip gloss on in my dressing room. When we went back out to the club somebody took our picture, and the next day it was all over the tabloids. That night ended up being a huge turning point in my career as a mini performer because suddenly Mini Britney was on TMZ with Lindsay Lohan. I didn't have a cell phone then, but somehow news channels and clubs all over

the country tracked down my home phone number and were calling wanting to interview me or book me to perform as Mini Britney. Literally overnight, I was getting stopped on the streets of Manhattan by people who recognized me as Mini Britney— it was that big on TMZ at the time.

The Box had originally hired me for one week, but after that night they extended it to two, and then every few months they'd fly me back out to New York to perform. I was making two grand a week, with all expenses paid, to perform at the hottest club in New York City. I remember at one point they even offered me an additional $500 to shave my head onstage in some kind of twisted pantomime of Britney's notorious meltdown. I wanted to say, "At least come to me with an offer of $1,000," but of course I turned them down. Overnight, I went from nobody knowing who I was to being in demand, not only all over the country, but all over the world.

|||||||||||||||||||||

MEANWHILE, MY RELATIONSHIP WITH JOE had been steadily evolving from a friendship to something more. I was still in San Antonio and he was living in Los Angeles, but we had started talking on the phone every day. We'd been attracted to each other since that night in Detroit back in 2000, and when Joe was filling in for Mini Kiss we knew we wanted to be together but we didn't know how or when. At that point, Joe was still in the same relationship he had been in when we had first met. I knew he wasn't happy, but he also wasn't quite ready to walk away either. I had been in a string of relationships with both average-sized and LP guys. I liked the security, so I would jump from one relationship to another, but I was also a wild child and I never wanted to be tied down so I never really fully committed to anyone. That year Joe and I finally found ourselves single at the same time and we jumped right into a very intense romance, but it was stressful almost from the get-go because we were coming into it with a lot of baggage.

When I moved back to LA from San Antonio, I stayed with Tonya until I got back on my feet. At that time, she was doing stand-in and stunt work for various television shows. Child labor laws limit the number of hours that children are allowed to work on set, so often they will hire LPs to stand-in for child actors. Tonya has done stand-in work on just about every show about an African American family on television from the past twenty years: *The Bernie Mac Show, Family Matters, The Hughleys*. Basically, if you were a black child actor, most likely at some point Tonya stood-in for you on set when you were a kid.

About a month after I moved back, I was offered a permanent headlining contract with Planet Hollywood for three grand a week at their club called Krave, which had a cabaret show called Little Legends. Joe had just come off doing *The Benchwarmers* with Adam Sandler and was waiting for his next big role to come in so I begged him to do Little Legends with me. He was in a good place with his career, but I was still trying to figure out what mine would be. He wasn't into the whole mini impersonation thing, but he agreed to do the show because he loved me and wanted to spend time with me. Since we would be working six days a week, and it didn't make sense to travel back and forth from LA, we rented a studio in Vegas off Sahara and Rainbow. It was attached to a house that was rented out by a rotating roster of roommates we almost never saw. Whoever had made the home addition must have had some kind of disability, because everything was very low and there were railings everywhere. This was both beneficial *and* annoying because although certain things—like kitchen counters—were at our height, other things were inconvenient, like the fact that the bathroom had a wheelchair-accessible, drive-in shower but no bathtub.

The best thing about that studio, though, was that it allowed pets so I was able to bring my dog to Vegas with me. Mahatma had come into my life while I was living in San Antonio. One afternoon, I was walking one of the rescue dogs that my mom was fostering at the time, and this scrappy little blue and white Chihuahua mix appeared out of nowhere and followed me all the way back to her house. I put up signs all over the neighborhood and when nobody called to claim him I took him to the vet to have him checked for a microchip. He wasn't chipped, but while we were there the vet discovered that his balls had never descended and they had become so infected that they had turned blue. My mom and I nursed Mahatma back to health,

Mahatma

and I got so attached that I decided to bring him with me when I moved back to LA. People always ask me if I chose the name because he was small, like Mahatma Rice, but my mom actually chose the name because it's the Sanskrit word for "great soul." Mahatma was so gentle, endearing, and loving that it was the perfect name for him.

Little Legends was an hour-long show—no intermission—of mini celebrity impersonators. The club was set up like an intimate cabaret style theater, so the audience sat at tables covered with white linen table clothes and little tea lights. In addition to Mini Britney, I got to do multiple characters: Mini Elton, Mini Cher, Mini Alanis—you name it, I did it. We had anywhere from five to seven LP performers doing impersonations of everyone from MC Hammer and Shakira, to Michael Jackson and Tina Turner. We even had our very own LP Elvis impersonator.

Little Legends is where I met Adams and Abdul Kone, two brothers from the Ivory Coast, with whom I ended up working for years after. They looked so much alike that everybody mistook them for twins—so much so, in fact, that we actually incorporated it into their act. We had them team up as Mini Michael Jackson and during "Bad" they would do this cool trick where Adams would be on stage in the spotlight, the lights would go dark, and when they came back up Abdul would be in a go-go box behind the audience at the back of the theater. Mini Michael Jackson would seem to have materialized behind them out of thin air like a cool magic trick.

The brothers were in their late thirties to early forties, but they looked like they were twenty. They could do all kinds of flips and acrobatics and had come to the US to tour with Univer-Soul Circus as part of this amazing troupe of African dancers. When they introduced me to the other people in their troupe,

it was: "This is my brother...this is my other brother...this is my cousin...this is my brother." Their father had forty-five kids (seven with their mother)—and of those seven, three had acromesomelia (acro, for short), which, as far as I know, is one of the only kinds of dwarfism where you see multiple siblings in one family with two average-sized parents. Other than their head size (which is typically average) the bodies of people with acro are relatively proportionate, so they are usually very athletic. People often confuse acros with pseudos because their facial features and bodies are so similar, but pseudos come with unfortunate hip and back issues (stenosis, scoliosis, kyphosis), whereas acros tend to have fewer health issues related to their dwarfism.

Going into the show it felt like we had been promised the world, but once we got to Vegas the production value for Little Legends turned out to be very limited; there was just one stagehand, one sound guy, and backstage we had one dressing room for the guys and one for the women. I already had my own costumes, but for most of the other mini impersonators there were little-to-no props or costumes. Adams and Abdul were performing as Mini MC Hammer in what they had brought with them, which basically was a couple of pairs of skin-tight black leggings—I mean, how can you do MC Hammer without harem pants? We were working with the bare minimum, but I was making enough headlining and didn't want the show to fall apart, so I ended up going to a local thrift shop to hunt down props and costumes. And *then* I paid to have them tailored to fit all our little people performers! I was particularly proud of a pair of gold-sequined, pleated shorts I found that, with a little tailoring, happened to work perfectly on the brothers as Hammer pants. I was determined to make it work,

so we basically financed the show ourselves in the hope that once it did well the producers would recognize the value of what they had.

Despite all that, I loved Little Legends because I was headlining and getting to do all these great characters, and the best part was that Joe and I got to perform together. He was Sonny to my Cher, and we were both in the Village People for the big finale. I had talked Tonya into doing the show as well, so on weekends she would drive out from LA to open the show as Mini Tina Turner. During the week Joe would open with a drum solo as Mini Tommy Lee. They actually wanted Joe to do more acts, but he wasn't really interested. Joe was more of an actor than a performer. Before (and after) Little Legends he was in a traveling production of *Mabou Mines DollHouse*, a deconstruction of the Ibsen classic in which all the male roles were performed by LP actors, so he wasn't exactly excited about doing celebrity impersonations in a Vegas cabaret show. But he knew how important Little Legends was to me, so he stuck it out way longer than he should have just to make me happy.

A few months into Little Legends, Joe surprised me with tickets to see Smashing Pumpkins (his all-time favorite band) at the Palms. On the way to the venue, he pulled over and put on "1979." When he got out of the car and asked me to dance, I was like, "Are you crazy?" But then he looked at me and out of the blue asked me to marry him. It was the most romantic moment of my life. I just remember feeling so in love with this man who hated dancing, but who was dancing with me to his favorite song on the side of the road. I was on cloud nine. The rest of the night is a blur, but I remember that we didn't really watch much of the concert that night because we were kissing the whole time.

That winter I gave up Radio City to stay with Little Legends, but Joe left Vegas to do Radio City in Phoenix and Costa Mesa. He didn't think Little Legends was a healthy environment for any of us, and I think he was just fed up with trying to make it work. Every couple of weeks our paychecks would bounce, but then a few days later they would clear. At that point, Tonya said, "I'm out." Every weekend for months she'd been driving out from LA, and it just got to the point where it wasn't worth it for her, financially or emotionally.

Without Tonya and Joe, trying to make the show work was more stressful than ever. Everybody was leaving and I was taking up the slack, so by then I was in every other number. I'd perform as Mini Britney, then run backstage and change into Mini Elton for the next number, then run backstage to put on my floor-length Mini Alanis wig, and so on for seven shows a week. I stayed, struggling to make it work through January, but after two paychecks bounced in a row, I told them, "Pay me in cash or I'm leaving." I remember they basically laughed at me because they didn't believe I would really walk away. That same day I went to the club, picked up every single prop and costume that I had bought and paid to have tailored, and I left. I had no clue what I was going to do next, but I knew there was no way I was going back to Little Legends. I felt the smartest move was to go back to California, so it was back to Los Angeles and the auditioning grind.

I stayed with Tonya again for a few weeks and then, when Joe finished Radio City, he and I moved into a one bedroom in North Hollywood together. Around that same time, an executive from A&E reached out to say they were interested in doing a show with me. I pitched them the idea of doing a behind-the-scenes reality show about a troupe of mini impersonators and they loved it. I interviewed with three different production companies, and ended up going with Left Right Productions, a New York-based production company that had done a bunch of shows with MTV and VH1. So, we went back to Vegas and I filmed a pilot with Joe, Tonya, the brothers, and a few of the other mini performers from Little Legends. My idea was to call it *Four Foot Two*, which I thought was a fun way of looking things. I thought absolutely the show would get picked up, but just as we were ready to pitch the pilot to A&E everything went "little." Suddenly, there was a flood of little people shows on cable (*Little People, Big World*, *Pit Boss*, *Little Chocolatiers*)—I like to joke that TLC should stand for the "The Little Channel"—so the network got cold feet and pulled out. I guess timing is everything. It was such a disappointment to get so close and have this opportunity slip through my fingers. After that I was still being approached regularly by production companies about doing a reality show, but you don't get paid to do shows that don't get picked up, so my attitude at that point was basically: "No thank you. I'm done with shows. I'm going to stick to touring."

|||||||||||||||||||||

AFTER JOE AND I MOVED to North Hollywood I decided to start volunteering at Forte Animal Rescue (a nonprofit dog rescue based out of Marina del Rey) as a way to keep my head together. We adopted a rescue named Bamboo, a wiry Jack Russell/Chihuahua mix, who cured Mahatma of his anxiety. Before we had Bamboo, whenever we went out Mahatma would always chew the doorframe to pieces or rip all the vertical blinds down because he couldn't stand to be alone. But, once we took in Bamboo, it calmed Mahatma and he was never afraid to be alone again.

I get my love of animals from my mom, who is a dedicated animal rights activist.

Rescuing strays is a passion I inherited from my mom. Despite the disconnect we have over my chosen career path, my mother is my best friend and I have a tremendous amount respect for her. She is the most dedicated person I have ever met. She volunteers with the Feral Cat Coalition and the Animal Defense League. Every day she is out there making the world a better place. Fostering and rescuing animals fulfills her need to care for and save the world. I feel like she is Superwoman for what she does. She's the reason I keep a leash and cat food in my car (because dogs like cat food better than dog food) in case I come across a stray that needs rescuing—which I have, several times.

After we moved back to LA, my relationship with Joe began to deteriorate. When he proposed to me back in Vegas we both thought we were ready and that this was our time, but in reality, we weren't and it wasn't. We had almost pulled the trigger while we were living in Vegas. I had booked a venue and put down a nonrefundable deposit, but one week before the wedding was supposed to happen Joe got cold feet and backed out. We had been planning for months, and then all of a sudden, he wanted to pump the breaks. He said it was because he wanted to wait until we could have a big wedding with both our families and all our friends, but deep down we both knew that we just weren't ready. At the time I was angry and hurt, but looking back now I know he was right to wait.

Joe was still in the process of moving all his stuff out of his ex's place, which definitely complicated things. In reality, neither one of us was ready to be in a new relationship, but we were acting like we were because we were very much in love with each other. He still needed closure with his ex and I felt like I was trying to get my career on track. I was still regularly touring as Mini Brittany, but I needed to figure out my next move.

CHAPTER SEVEN

THE M-WORD

I was so proud of myself when I finally landed my first lead role in an independent feature film. I would be playing Leanne, a nice Christian girl who boosts the morale of her fellow little people and spurs them on to beat a team of average-sized mascots in a competition for a $1,000,000 inheritance left by an eccentric former mascot turned porn mogul. This was the first time that I had a feature-length script with pages and pages of lines to memorize and I could not have been more thrilled. Never mind that it was going to be a low-budget, crude, and often downright offensive film. Never mind that it would feature a scene in which I had to (simulate) explosive diarrhea and (actually) vomit in a crowded restaurant. Never mind that the word "midget" (which is degrading and offensive to people with dwarfism) appeared liberally throughout the script—no, the story ended with a positive message in which little people win the competition and teach their average-sized competitors that height has nothing to do with heart. I decided that *this* was going to be my big shot.

When I was called in to read for the director, the waiting room outside his office was filled with dozens of LP and average-sized actors, some of whom had gone all out in mascot costumes. (There was a taco, two knights in shining armor, at least one alligator, and a girl who, for some reason, was dressed like Wendy—from the fast-food chain of the same name—in a blue-and-white gingham pinafore, red pigtails, and freckles.) I remember looking around the room and thinking: *Only in Hollywood.* Joe had auditioned as well, although when he got the call that he had landed role of Geoffrey, an over-the-top, campy gay character complete with beret and side neck scarf, he wasn't quite as psyched as I was. I personally thought the wardrobe was hilarious, though Joe didn't quite see it that way.

Tribute to Big Red was to be filmed in Texas in the middle of summer, so Joe and I transported our lives to a room at the Residence Inn in Dallas. At this point, we had been dating for about a year and we were supposed to be engaged, but instead of planning a wedding we were at each other's throats every single day. Without giving ourselves time to heal from the past, we jumped into working on this film together, and we found ourselves holed up in a cramped hotel room for two and a half months with two dogs, ten years of relationship baggage between us, and nowhere to escape.

Living and working together (all day, every day) for the entire summer tested our relationship daily because we never had any alone time. It didn't help matters that I had my first onscreen kiss, a cheesy make-out scene with one of the average-sized actors in the film. The guy was happily married, and I was totally in love with Joe, but there was still a lot of tension and weird jealousy. When we were filming the scene, Joe kept wisecracking and making comments like, "Most people don't have their mouths wide open when they kiss onscreen." He was being such a nuisance that the producers offered to take him out for a drink just to get him off the set.

I probably should have known that the film was in trouble when Gary Coleman was the most famous actor in the movie. More than any of us, Gary hated doing this film. I remember he would blatantly cuss out the producers and director in front of the rest of the cast on a daily basis. He was having marital and health issues, and he just seemed completely miserable the entire time we were shooting. I remember at one point, we were actually told to make him mad so that they could film his reaction, so when you see Gary pissed off in the movie more often than not he was pissed off in real life. I think the scene he hated the most was a nude scene where he was wearing a prosthesis that made him look like he had a huge dong. I heard that after filming wrapped, he fought with the producers to have that scene removed, but he wasn't successful. I felt horrible for Gary because he seemed so tortured and unhappy. Every day we were on set he was fighting with his wife and battling with the producers—all while undergoing painful weekly dialysis treatments.

During the filming of *Tribute to Big Red*, the script required that we participate in a series of challenges that ranged from ridiculous to downright humiliating. We were making this movie in the style of MTV's *Jackass* and Sacha Baron Cohen's *Borat*, which were huge hits at the time, so while we were filming these challenges the people around us didn't necessarily know that they were witnessing a scripted situation. We did a scene on the Ranger's baseball field where we had to try to run around all the bases without security tackling us. Joe (who has spine and hip issues related to his pseudoachondroplasia) didn't want to jack up his body running, so he sat down on home plate and

High-jump challenge, on the set of *Tribute to Big Red.*

made snow angels in the dirt. I think I made it to first base and then immediately was escorted off the field. When the local rodeo came through town, we filmed one scene for the competition where each team had to attempt to catch a greased pig and another where we played Rodeo Roulette, which basically meant we had to sit at a table playing cards while a charging bull was set free into the arena; the last person to leave the table, won.

Right from the get-go all the LPs in the cast had issues with what we were being asked to do. We all knew when we signed on to do the movie that there were going to be scenes that pushed the boundaries of what we considered offensive, but there were certain things in the script that we felt went too far, such as a naked locker-room shower scene for the male LPs (that we negotiated to a covered-towel, locker-room shower scene) and a diaper (yes, *diaper)* scene that was never to see the light of day. We banded together and refused to do certain things, and though we were able to tone down some of the most offensive stuff in the script, I'm pretty sure that my puking/diarrhea scene was more than enough embarrassment for all little people everywhere.

The filmmakers took their explosive diarrhea seriously and to make scene look as realistic as possible, they had rigged up this contraption that was basically constructed of a long clear tube stuffed down my pants, which was connected to an IV sack filled with chocolate milk, coffee grounds, and what looked like rancid cottage cheese taped under my shirt, which in turn was connected to an enormous CO2 tank hidden from camera under the table. I can't remember exactly *what* the motivation for this scene was—my guess is they just thought it would be awesome to see a little person crap her pants on camera—but they also wanted one of us to throw up; it didn't really matter who (but it would be great if somebody actually managed to throw up *on* me.) As "incentive" they offered a hundred dollars in cash to whomever puked first and to help us along they had each of us each drink a gallon of chocolate milk. Then they just let the cameras roll. After ten or fifteen minutes of chugging down warm, sickly-sweet, syrupy milk, I'm not too proud to say that *I* won that hundred-dollar prize.

After I puked, I started running towards the door. My character was supposed to be embarrassed (no problem summoning that emotion) because the man that I was love with had just seen me puke (which, actually, he just had), so as soon as I threw up I started running towards the door. Just as I got there they triggered their contraption. All of a sudden, I felt like I had been spanked with a wet, rolled-up towel as a liquid concoction of coffee grounds, curdled chocolate milk, and cottage cheese shot out of my ass like a rocket! And all over this nice family restaurant where we were shooting this particular gem of a scene. Let's just say, it got distance. The owners of the restaurant were also producers of the film, so the people sitting nearest our table were hired extras, but the people a couple of rows over had no idea we were filming a movie (and at that point I doubt even the extras had any idea why my butt was exploding all over their tables). Not only did I win the hundred-dollar prize, I actually got stunt pay for that scene. So there's that, at least.

I knew the movie wasn't going to win any awards for me, but the experience meant a lot to me at the time. I felt like this was just the beginning, that bigger and better things were on the horizon for me. Through my rose-colored glasses, I kept telling myself all the humiliation, the strain on my relationship with Joe, and the physical pain from the stunts would all be worth it once the movie was released.

||||||||||||||||||||||

AFTER FILMING WRAPPED, JOE AND I moved into an apartment in Fullerton. He went back to auditioning for acting roles and I went back to touring as Mini Britney. About month later, our lives were just getting back to normal when Joe got a call from one of our fellow cast members. When the phone rang, we were hanging out in our living room playing chess—I was destroying him, of course (I remember that part very clearly). When Joe picked up the phone, the smile on his face changed to a look that was a mix of outrage and disbelief. When he got off the phone, he said, "You are never going to believe what happened."

I'm naturally curious, and judging by the look on Joe's face this was a piece of juicy gossip, so I couldn't wait to hear what he had to say.

"The producers changed the name of the movie from *Tribute to Big Red* to *Midgets vs. Mascots*."

My mouth dropped. I couldn't believe it. How could this have happened? During filming we'd had multiple meetings about how offensive the M-word is to little people. For us, this word comes from a dark place. Historically, it has ties to P.T. Barnum who used it to promote his use of little people in freak shows for public amusement. Need I say more? Using the M-word is demoralizing because it chips away at our humanity and reduces us to something that people don't have to respect. I would never have agreed to do the movie if I had suspected that they would put the word "midget" in the title.

Once word got out that they had changed the title, every LP in the film was furious. One cast member even fought to have his name taken off the movie on IMDB. Even the average-sized actors who had played the mascots called us to say how bad they felt about the title change—after spending two months working with us, and how vocal we had been about the M-word, they had come to understand how deeply offensive that word is to us. That night, Joe called the director and cussed him out so badly he scared even me. The director insisted that he had no control over the title and that it was the *producers* who had made the decision to change it. We even called the Screen Actors Guild to complain, but we were told that there was nothing we could do because the original title was a "working title" and therefore it was within the filmmakers' legal rights to change it.

What I heard later was that a year before we signed on to do the movie there had been a script circulating with the title

Midgets vs. Mascots. There had been an open audition but, of course, not one single little person showed up. The speculation now was that the filmmakers had changed the name, held another audition, and sure enough, tons of aspiring LP actors (myself included) showed up this time, all eagerly clutching our headshots for a chance at a feature that at least ended (despite its many other flaws) with a positive message for our community. Man, were we suckers.

A few months later, in early 2009, Joe and I found out through our agents that *Midgets vs. Mascots* had been selected for the Tribeca Film Festival. I remember thinking, *What? That piece of shit movie was selected?* The next day my cell phone rang and I recognized the number as one of producers from the movie. I had no interest in speaking to him so I let it go to voicemail. In his message, he said they wanted to pay for us to come to New York to promote the film during the festival; I thought he must be out of his mind. I never called him back, and Joe and I continued to ignore every call we received for weeks. I *should* have been overjoyed that a movie I was in had been selected for the Tribeca Film Festival. I had dreamed of a moment like this since I was a little girl...but this was nothing like what I had imagined it would be.

A few weeks later, I was walking down Sunset Boulevard after a fun night out with my girls. I had a Mini Britney gig coming up and I was blasting "Circus" through my earbuds, so I was in my own little world. Out of nowhere this big black SUV pulled over to the side of the curb and practically ran me over. I could sense that the driver had rolled down the window and was calling to me, but my first thought was: *Stranger danger! Stranger danger!* I decided not to engage and kept walking. A few moments later, the same SUV pulled into the gas station right in front to me. Then the director of (the-movie-formerly-known-as) *Tribute to Big Red* got out of the car and said, "Terra, I'm so glad I ran into you."

At first he tried to play it smooth and make small talk, about his wife being pregnant and how random it was that he ran into me on his way to the Home Depot.

"Did you hear about Tribeca?" he asked, finally getting to the point.

"Yes, but with the title change, I really don't think it's something I want to be a part of," I told him.

For the next fifteen minutes, he did his best to convince me that the movie was about so much more than the title, that it conveyed the message that "midget" is an offensive and derogatory word, and that everyone would see that message beyond the comedy in it all. As he went on to rave about my performance, saying things you'd only expect your publicist to say about you, I had a flash of...*maybe*. He gave me his card before driving off, and I told him I'd let him know.

I was disgusted about the title change and felt they had lied to us, but at the same time there was a part of me that felt like this couldn't have all been for nothing.

Anyone who knows me knows that I believe everything happens for a reason. I'm the audience for *The Secret*. I'm a vision-board-creating, sign-embracing type of girl. I had been ignoring calls from the producer, I was ready to boycott the premiere, and then out of the blue I ran into the director on his way to the Home Depot. What were the chances? That encounter was so bizarre and unexpected that I began to feel like it was meant to be—like the universe was trying to tell me something. This was a sign. It had to be.

In the end, Joe and I decided to go to New York. We were still angry, but we felt if we went to the festival we could at least have some control over the message that was being put out there about the movie. This was my first red carpet experience and, even though the circumstances weren't ideal, I wanted to enjoy it a little. So I decided to go all out and have a dress made for the event. On the night of the premier, from the moment we stepped out of the car it felt like total insanity. Paparazzi were screaming our names and asking us to pose; I couldn't even see their faces because there were so many flashes going off. It was a big event, with lots of industry people and sports agents, and I remember everything being very bright. The mascots walked the red carpet in costume, and even Gary Coleman and Ron Jeremy (who had a cameo in the film) were there. Joe was not taking it seriously at all; he kept grabbing my ass as we walked the carpet, so we looked about as mature as the film we were there to promote. The whole night was very surreal. Whenever anyone asked me about the movie, the first words out of my mouth were: "I do not support the title."

After the red carpet, we went to the screening. Tribeca was billing the movie as "outrageous and hilarious" and "a cross between *Jackass* and the *Real World/Road Rules Challenge*." Watching the movie, I felt like it had its funny moments, but most of the time I was appalled by what I saw because so much of it fed into the cruelest stereotypes of little people. During filming, we had truly hoped that that the positive message at the end of the film would redeem all the negative stereotypes and offensive jokes, but when they changed the title they ended up reinforcing everything that we were against. At the end of the screening, the PR people gave out little questionnaires to everyone in the audience, and I totally trashed the movie.

Somehow, I have no clue how, *Midgets vs. Mascots* went on to win third place in the Heineken Audience Choice Award at the festival—perhaps the voters were oversampling their Heinekens.

CHAPTER EIGHT

HOUSE OF T-PAIN

After Tribeca, I went back to touring as Mini Britney and audi-tioning for character work. That year I was a baby bear in a Kellogg's commercial. It was filmed on the Universal lot and basically involved jumping out of a minivan and running into a store, where I devoured my bowl of cereal. I also did a couple of episodes for an online educational show called *Buddy Bear*. This time I was (you guessed it) a baby bear. I had experience with full costume work, but the head alone weighed thirty-five pounds because it had these mechanical eyes. I had to wear an earpiece to communicate with the crew because I couldn't hear anything inside the costume. We did about eight three-minute episodes, and I think they tried to pitch it to Nickelodeon, but nothing ever came of it.

Thankfully, my next big break was just around the corner. In December, I got a call from Adams and Abdul, who were down in Atlanta getting ready to go on tour with T-Pain, who was opening for Lil Wayne's I Am Music Tour. It was a massive oper-ation with multiple opening acts, including Keyshia Cole, Keri

Hilson, and Gym Class Heroes. For his show, T-Pain had a circus theme and he had brought the brothers onto the tour (along with fire performers, clowns, contortionists, and stilt walkers) after he had seen them perform with UniverSoul. Knowing that T-Pain had produced a couple of Britney tunes, the brothers told him about my act and he loved the idea of bringing Mini Britney onto the tour.

When I got the call I was psyched. Even though I wouldn't be bringing in what I could have earned touring as Mini Britney on my own, the I Am Music Tour would be playing huge arenas all over North America. It would be a whole new level of exposure for me. A few days later I flew down to Atlanta, T-Pain's hometown, where rehearsals for the tour were already underway.

Those first two weeks in Atlanta were incredibly stressful because you never knew from one day to the next if you were going to get cut. They were bringing in new talent every day, and if Pain didn't like what he saw in rehearsals you'd be told to pack your bags and go home. At one point, they fired three different contortionists in three days, and in the two weeks I was there they sent home seven out of ten dancers. I'd heard they had fired two other LP performers before I got there, so everybody thought I'd be gone before rehearsals were over; for a while, I had to agree.

We spent all day learning the dance routines. Because Pain liked to switch up the songs in his set, we had to be able to do the same choreography to different music at a moment's notice. I just remember the choreographer yelling at us all the time: "No, no, no! Run it again—and this time dance with *rhythm*!" Somehow, I made it through rehearsals, and when the tour kicked off in Miami that December I got my first taste of what it was like to perform in front of ten thousand-plus screaming fans.

I was in a group number and the finale; I even had a little solo moment. About halfway into the show T-Pain would stop the music and tell the crowd he was bringing out a very special guest. Britney Spears had just put out *Circus* and he made it sound like he was bringing her out on the stage to join *his* circus. Then *I* would come out in my skintight, red vinyl "Oops! I Did It Again" catsuit, do a little dance, and shake my booty. Then the brothers would help me break the catsuit away to reveal a sparkly black bikini like the one Britney had infamously worn at the 2007 VMAs. I danced and shook my booty some more, then blew the audience a kiss before strutting off stage. It was a funny little moment in the show and the audience always went bananas.

Karl Giant

A couple of weeks into the tour, I got a call from my manager that Britney's people had reached out to say she was interested in bringing me on her upcoming Circus Tour as Mini Britney. I was beyond excited, but once they found out I was touring as Mini Britney with T-Pain the offer vanished. It was such a disappointment to lose that opportunity. As much as I was enjoying touring with T-Pain, it would have been amazing to perform as Mini Britney alongside the pop princess herself.

The tour rolled on through Houston, Dallas, Detroit, Chicago, and Washington DC. Our buses were kept fully stocked at all times with bottles of Hennessy and Nuvo. It was a nonstop party, and best of all Mini Britney was a hit everywhere we went. Nicki Minaj, who had just been discovered by Lil Wayne, was a singer in his entourage; she was still just a young girl trying to make it as a performer. She brought this adorable little Yorkshire terrier on tour with her. In New Orleans, Lil Wayne's hometown, every single person in the audience was wearing red, and we're talking a sold-out show of over 17,000 people. You looked out from the stage and it was just a massive sea of red. I'd never seen anything like it. It was definitely a surreal experience.

On December 31, we were back in Atlanta for a New Year's Eve performance at the Philips Arena. After the show, we celebrated the countdown to midnight in the hotel lobby and toasted the New Year with solo cups of champagne. Then Pain had a couple of cars pick us all up and bring us back to his house for a private, after-hours party. All day people had been whispering about how they'd heard that T-Pain had hired special performers for the evening, which made me worry we might be getting replaced.

When we arrived at T-Pain's house we were immediately escorted down a flight of stairs that led into his very own, private, subterranean nightclub. Where the rest of his place looked just like a typical suburban house, Pain's basement was something straight out of an episode of *MTV Cribs*—in fact, his crib *was* featured during Season 16 and I assure you "Club Nappy Boy" was a highlight of the episode. In addition to several recording studios, all with state-of-the-art equipment, Pain had his very own ultra-exclusive club, complete with a fiber-optic stripper

Chillin' on T-Pain's tour bus.

pole, DJ stand, wall to wall flat-screen TVs, and a fully loaded bar. There were even separate men's and women's restrooms.

As we crossed the threshold into Club Nappy Boy, we were each handed $300 dollars in one-dollar bills. When T-Pain called in his "entertainers" for the night, what seemed like hundreds of strippers of all shapes and flavors flooded into the club. There was only about thirty of us from the tour, and we were easily outnumbered by strippers five to one. Some people immediately threw all their money up into the air at all once, which basically caused of frenzy of half-naked, glitter-covered strippers slapping into one another as they scrambled on all fours to grab up the bills. I remember they were all carrying these little tote bags, and they were stuffing as much money into them as they could. Some of the women from the tour were reluctant to part with their wads of singles, so the stage manager kept coming around and saying, "That money is supposed to go to the strippers. Stop stuffing those bills in your bra."

Towards the end of the night, T-Pain got on the mic and announced he had one last surprise. Then he called me and the brothers over and someone handed him three huge stacks of cash; it must have been at least three or four grand in total. Pain gave one stack to Adams, one to Abdul, and the last stack to me. All of sudden, there was a stampede of strippers coming straight at us. I barely had time to process what had just happened before there were booties and titties smacking me in the face. I was a little terrified, but the brothers totally loved it. It was the craziest, most insane, naked, vulgar, hilarious, and entertaining night of my life. (Luckily, no little people or strippers were harmed in the making of this evening.)

Less than a month later we found ourselves looking forward to an entirely different kind of celebration. On January 20, the day Barack Obama was to be sworn in as the 44th president of the United States, our tour bus was traveling from Worcester, Massachusetts, across the border into Canada for a show in Calgary on January 22. The plan was to cross the border and get to the hotel in Calgary with enough time to watch the inauguration on live television along with the rest of the country. We had heard that an estimated 1.8 million people were flooding onto the National Mall to witness and celebrate this profound historic moment. For me, the day had special significance because under this new administration, for the first time, little people would have access to affordable healthcare.

About an hour from the checkpoint one of the tour managers came onto our bus and told everybody to put whatever drugs they had (and for the record I had nothing) into a bag, which he then threw out the window—it doesn't take a genius to figure out that a tour bus was wrapped with the image of two African American males drinking Nuvo and smoking a blunt is going raise some suspicion at the border. When we got to the Canadian border, they had us all line up on the side of the road while they searched the bus. The temperature outside was below freezing and it was snowing, but they wouldn't let us back on for hours. They brought in drug sniffing dogs to inspect the bus and wanted to know where each of us slept—they even pulled off our sheets and took our mattresses out of our bunks.

In the end, after border patrol scoured every inch of our bus, they found one tiny roach in this girl's bunk (which she had forgotten she even had), and over $50,000 in cash that one of the guys on tour had won gambling in a casino New Orleans. You're supposed to declare anything over $10,000, and if he had just thought to split up the money up and let a few of us hold smaller amounts for him it would have been fine, but because he kept it all he ended up having to pay a huge fine. One guy was flagged because he hadn't been paying his child support, another guy couldn't cross because of a DUI on his record, and Adams and Abdul couldn't cross with their Ivory Coast passports—we were losing people left and right. In the end, the brothers, roach girl, deadbeat dad, and DUI guy had to take a taxi to the nearest airport and fly home on their own dime. As for the rest of us, instead of watching Obama's inauguration from the comfort of a Canadian hotel room, we were stuck at border control for five hours and ended up missing one of the most historic moments of our lives.

CHAPTER NINE

ON MY OWN

It's always a big adjustment coming home after being on the road for months. You live in such a bubble when you're out on tour that it's easy to become disconnected from your real life. So much so, that you can come home to find that you feel like you don't belong there anymore. I was originally only supposed to be gone for a month and half, but the I Am Music Tour was so successful it was extended through April 2009, so I ended up being on tour for 5 months. Sadly, because I had booked a job in New York before the tour was extended, I had to leave a day early and didn't get to be in the last show. The experience ended very abruptly for me and when I got back home to LA my life there felt as if it didn't fit me anymore.

On top of that, I had lost my beloved Mahatma. When I left for the tour, I had taken Bamboo and Mahatma to my mom in San Antonio. But a few days later, she called to tell me that Mahatma was sick. Out of the blue he had started losing muscle mass right above his eye. The vet diagnosed him with masticatory muscle myositis, an inflammatory disease the attacks the muscles in the face, mainly those used for chewing. We had no idea what had caused it, but it spread so fast that within days Mahatma had lost all the muscle function in his entire face. He couldn't open or close his mouth to eat or drink, so my mom hand-fed him wet food, and helped him chew. The vet gave him steroid shots to reduce the inflammation and assured us that Mahatma would recover, but the disease began to spread through his entire body. It was heartbreaking. He couldn't even come back home to Los Angeles with me because the vet wouldn't approve him to fly. In the end, Mahatma was in so much pain that my mom had to put him to sleep.

On top of being heartbroken over Mahatma, my relationship with Joe was deteriorating to the point where we were barely getting along. Joe hadn't worked for a year, and the stress of that was really getting to him. He'd say he needed to go pick up some things from his ex's house and then he'd spend the night there. I knew what was going on, but I never said anything— partly because I knew in my heart of hearts that Joe wasn't over his ex, but also because I was keeping my own secret. While I was on tour, I had been swept up in the excitement of being on the road and had behaved like a dumb little girl in need of atten- tion. There are very few choices I've made in life that I can't live with, but I would take back cheating on Joe in a heartbeat if I could. I never wanted to be *that* girl, but I was, and to this day I regret my reckless behavior.

Neither one of us wanted to admit to being unfaithful so the tension between us just kept building. We were in love and we kept trying to make things work, but we just weren't ready. Neither one of us was happy, which made us very dysfunc- tional. It had gotten to the point where it wasn't healthy for us to stay together. I had never lived on my own and I was craving

that that sense of freedom and independence that I had felt on tour. So, without even telling Joe, I started looking for my own place. I signed a lease and put down a deposit on an apartment in Hollywood. When I was ready to move out, I took Joe to a diner (that, weirdly, was called Joe's) and gave him back my key to our apartment. I cried through the whole dinner and I knew I was being a bitch, but I felt in my gut that it was what I needed at that point in my life. Joe was surprised and hurt, but I think on some level he knew I was right to move out. I'm not proud of how I handled things, but I was convinced that what I needed was to be on my own, and I didn't want Joe to talk me out of it.

||||||||||||||||||||

MY NEW APARTMENT, A ONE-BEDROOM on the second floor with a balcony, was right off Cherokee Avenue in the heart of Holly-wood. I felt like I was really in center of it all. My attitude was, if you're not on Sunset or Hollywood Boulevard on Friday and Saturday night then you're not out. In reality, the neighborhood was infested with tourists, twenty-year-olds, panhandlers, and homeless people, but to me it felt full of excitement and possibility. At least five times a week you'd hear police helicopters overhead. One time a guy who was being chased by the cops actually climbed up my balcony and ran through my apartment while I stood there in my pajamas, peeing in my pants. Another time I was dropping some packages off at the post office just down the street from my apartment and there was a woman sitting spread-eagle by the door. At first I wasn't sure if she was just scratching, but then this guy who was about to walk into the post office dropped his cell phone, turned right around, and walked as fast as he could in the other direction. I was on the phone with my agent, and said to him, "I'm pretty sure there's a homeless chick getting off in front of my post office."

The struggle of living paycheck to paycheck, trying to move my career forward, and the stress of seeing my bank account balance shrink down to nothing between gigs was rough, and now that I was living on my own I was solely responsible for my rent and bills. I was a total thrift shop junkie, so when I wasn't doing Mini Britney my biggest income came from hunting for designer purses and then reselling them on eBay. I loved the thrill of the hunt, and the rush of finding a genuine designer purse among racks of old junk; it's like finding a glistening diamond in a pile of coal. I became such a frequent customer, the thrift shops all knew me buy name. The most popular items I sold, where I knew I would get a good return on my investment, were signature pieces by Louis Vuitton. Typically, if you go to a thrift shop they don't know if the Louis Vuittons are real or fake. They can't be bothered to sort through them, so they sell all of them for $200. If you

Karl Giant

know what you're looking for you can double or even quadruple that money online because, on average, a genuine Louis Vuitton will sell for between $500 and $900. The most money I ever got was for a two-piece set of Louis Vuitton luggage. They were totally beat up; the linings were ripped and the big piece had a huge stain. I thought *maybe* I could make a hundred bucks resale because the shipping alone was a hundred, but I ended up making a little over $1,200 in all. That was a great week. I still have my eBay store and it costs $80 a month to keep it, but I always feel like anything can change at any moment and it's something I can always go back to if the entertainment work dries up.

After I split up with Joe, I think my mom figured I wasn't going to be able to make it on my own and that I'd end up moving back to San Antonio again. I am a big believer in channeling your energy toward realizing life goals. You have to be out there in the world believing in your dreams, *and* working hard at making them come true. My mother is more practical and down to earth. She believes in stability, consistency, and security (sometimes I wonder if she gave me my name to keep me grounded to the earth.) Although she definitely worries about me because she feels there's a lack of opportunities for little people in the entertainment industry, she wouldn't be happy with this career no matter my size; she'd only be slightly less worried if I were of average size. She knows nothing about the entertainment world and it scares the *bidillies* out of her.

My mother gave me a great foundation for life. I have every tool I could possibly need to be a successful independent woman, but because I never went back to school I will always feel like I let her down. She doesn't approve of the industry I work in, so no matter how successful I am, I will always have this need to impress her and make her proud of me to prove that I made the right choice.

Even though we both knew she was assuming I'd eventually come home, my mom and I talked on the phone every day and she tried her best to be supportive. I was still touring and doing impersonations, but I was really searching for what my next move would be. Most of the time I was making decent money impersonating or through Radio City, but the work was inconsistent. Sometimes I'd be booked twice in a week, sometimes, only once a month or every couple of months. I had to learn how to budget my money and live off what I had when the work wasn't out there.

My mom wasn't crazy about my plan to support myself with side jobs and the eBay store, but I wasn't about to give up on my dream. For the first time in my life I was living on my own and supporting myself. I felt I was on a path. I wasn't sure where that path was leading, but I knew it wasn't leading back to San Antonio.

CHAPTER TEN

OKLAHOMA

Once I started having success as Mini Britney, I began adding more characters to my repertoire. I did Mini Katy Perry and Mini Madonna, but my absolute favorite performer to impersonate was Lady Gaga because she's so theatrical. I felt such an affinity with her as an artist and I loved the challenge of trying to replicate her outrageous outfits, costumes, and stage sets.

Within a year, of moving into my own place, I was getting booked to perform all over the country (the only state I've never toured is Alaska) and for crazy gigs all over the world—Germany, Switzerland, Sweden, and England. At that point, I was working about three jobs a month, and getting paid anywhere between $200 to $1,500 for a gig in the States and upwards of $8,000 if I was hired to perform abroad. I still had lean times when I wasn't getting booked, so international work was the best because I could live for months off just a couple of days' work. At one point, I got paid twelve grand for two days' work performing as Mini Gaga on a German talent show called Das Superstars. I sang a medley of three songs and destroyed

Karl Giant

a miniature piano onstage. I don't speak a word of German, so when the judges were critiquing my performance I had no clue what they were saying, but I wasn't exactly heartbroken when I was eliminated in the first round.

In Hollywood, when it rains it pours, and just when I had been offered my biggest paycheck yet, to perform as Mini Britney at a club in Istanbul, I got a call that Johnny Knoxville was looking for a cute little person to play Jason Acuña's (aka Wee Man's) girlfriend for a scene in *Jackass 3D*. The director had seen me on social media as Mini Britney and thought I'd be great for the part. I was definitely nervous about taking the job because it was *Jackass*. They are known for doing insane stunts and disgusting things like eating their own vomit. (I had already done my fair share of vomiting on camera and was not looking to repeat the performance.) I was nervous about what they were going to ask me to do, but when they explained that we would be filming a fake scenario in a real environment (no vomit involved, whatsoever), I felt much better about it. This

Egan O'Keefe

was at the peak of their popularity, so *Jackass* was a huge opportunity, but they were shooting the same week I was to go to
Istanbul to perform as Mini Britney and I needed the income
from that job to cover me for the rest of the year. Thankfully, I
have an awesome manager who was able to negotiate changing
the dates in Istanbul for slightly less money, so I was able to do
both jobs.

We filmed in three bars around the city and the only other
people who knew what was going on were the owners. The crew
would hide cameras around the bar overnight, so none of the
staff or any of the customers would have any idea when we
came in that they were filming. The set-up for our scene was
that Jason and I were out on a date and then my "ex" would
walk in and discover I was out with some new guy. He would
confront us and then a physical altercation would ensue. It
went something like this:

Ex: (screaming) Terra, what fuck are you doing?

Terra: (mortified) Shh, calm down.

Jason: Who are you?

Ex: I'm her frickin' boyfriend, asshole.

Jason: That's cool, bud. I'm her man friend.

Ex: You know what? Fuck both of you.

Then my ex would leave the bar and come back a minute later with a couple of his LP buddies. He would shove Jason and then they would all get into a good old-fashioned, knock-down-drag-out barroom brawl. There were fake bottles planted around the bars, so they'd be smashing one another over the head with them, and then LP cops would storm in to break up the fight. The scene would end with a couple of LP paramedics carrying one of my ex's cronies out on a stretcher. The whole thing would escalate so quickly that the customers in the bar almost didn't have time to react.

Even though it may seem like the stunts or scenes in *Jackass* are insane and spontaneous, it's actually all handled very professionally and as a performer you feel safe. There were stunt coordinators on set and we were given a safe word to use if we were ever in pain or felt like we were in a sketchy situation. If you watch the movie, there's a scene where Johnny Knoxville is being chased by a dog. To get away he climbs up a telephone pole and the dog jumps up and latches his teeth onto Johnny's ass. At which point, you can hear Johnny Knoxville screaming "OKLAHOMA!!! OKLAHOMA!!!"

At the very first place we filmed, there was a guy sitting at the bar who engaged us as soon as we sat down. "Jason! Remember me? We went to high school together." Jason gave me a look, like he had no idea who this guy was, but that would happen to

Me with my amazing manager, Roy Rosental.

him all the time so we didn't think much of it—keep in mind we were in a bar in San Pedro at 11 o'clock in the morning, so you know these people are special. We continued with the scene and my "ex" came in and confronted us. When he left to go get his "buddies," the guy at the bar, who still thought he knew Jason, leaned over and said to him, "Don't worry, man. If he comes back, I'm packing." Immediately, Jason and I both shouted: "Oklahoma! Oklahoma! Oklahoma!"

On *Jackass*, more than any other movie that I've done, I felt I was part of a big family. It was close-knit group of kids and a lot of them have known one another since high school so they were all very close and in tune with one another. The wrap party was held at club on Hollywood and Highland. They had done the place up like the intro to the movie, so the décor was basically as if Rainbow Bright and My Little Pony gave birth to a Care Bear. There was free booze for the cast and crew all night, but our options were wine, Champagne, and beer. I never drink Champagne, but I knew enough that you don't normally drink it out of wine glasses filled to the top. There was a live rock band and everybody knew the words to their songs but me; I'm pretty sure that it was a big, well-known band, but I have no clue because by that point I had knocked back at least three or four wine glasses full of Champagne.

The last thing I remember clearly is being at the wrap party feeling fun and carefree as I danced the night away with the cast and crew. Then nothing, until I came to in my car somewhere around 3:00 am. I was parked at a meter, puking my guts out, and a cop was asking me if was okay. There was puke on me, puke all over my car, puke on the side of the road. I was so out of it I refused to take a Breathalyzer, so they took me down to the station. Because I admitted I was driving, they charged me with a DUI. They took my clothes and put me in these scrubs that didn't fit me at all, so they used an old pair of scissors to cut down the arms and legs. They did such a raggedy job that not only was I now in jail, I looked like I was in a homeless person in jail.

By the time they put me in a cell it must have been 4:00 or 5:00 in the morning. I just wanted to sleep, so I collapsed onto the nearest empty cot. Just as I was closing my eyes, I heard the most disgusting sound. There was no bathroom in the cell, just a stall in the corner with no door. I looked up and there was a woman sitting on the toilet, who by the sound of it was clearly having serious digestive issues. Then all of a sudden, she started puking. She must have thought she was done with whatever was happening on the toilet, because as she turned around to finish throwing up, a stream of diarrhea came shooting out of her ass. There was vomit and shit everywhere. A cop wheeled in a bucket of murky grey water, handed her a mop, and told her to clean up the mess, though all that really did was trap us in the cell with an aroma that I can only describe as a medley of industrial strength bleach, human feces, and vomit.

There were four of us in this cell, and when morning came one of the other girls, a pretty, skinny Hispanic chick, was released with me. Before the police give you back your clothes and driver's license, you have to stand in line to have your mug shot taken. When we were done, and we were getting back into our own clothes, my cellmate turned to me and asked, "Do I look like a hooker?" I guess when you've spent the night in a jail cell with someone, a question like that doesn't seem so odd. She was wearing a skintight dress, fishnet stockings, and 5-inch heels. *Hell yeah, you look like a hooker!* She explained that her fiancé was picking her up but he didn't know she was a prostitute, and she didn't think this was the best way for him to find out. I told her, "The fishnets and heels gotta go." She was definitely better off in just the dress and bare feet.

In the end, my license was suspended, I was ordered to pay $10,000 in fines, I had to attend sixteen mandatory AA meetings and three months of sobriety classes, and I had to complete thirty hours of community service. During the sobriety classes, they basically made us watch episode after episode of *Intervention*, which is a documentary series exactly about what its name suggests. Originally, they wanted me to do my community service at the Goodwill near my apartment, but since I knew everyone who worked there, I didn't want them to know I'd spent the night in jail. So, I ended up cleaning up trash on the side of the freeway. It was still local enough that I worried someone I knew would recognize me, so I disguised myself by wearing a hat so nobody could recognize me, though I'm not sure how inconspicuous you can be when you're a little person in a giant straw hat picking up trash by the side of the road.

CHAPTER ELEVEN

LITTLE PEOPLE PROBLEMS

The moment that Lady Gaga and Beyoncé released "Telephone" I called Tonya up and was like, "*Girl*, we have to do Mini Gaga and Mini Beyoncé." It was such a perfect fit. Entertainment is all about timing, and the timing couldn't have been more perfect for us. We came up with choreography for a 45-minute act with multiple characters and costume changes that was perfect for a theater show. If we were at a club we'd do a 7-minute medley and for or the last two songs Tonya would come out as Mini Beyoncé and the crowd would go crazy. We were like drag queens, but with more makeup and costume changes. One of our first gigs was at a minor-league ball field in New Orleans, where 5,000 people came to see us perform. From there we were working jobs all over the country. We performed in every US city from Seattle to Miami; we even did a show in Mexico together.

About a year later I was hired to perform as Mini Gaga at an event in New York City for the Wilhelmina modeling agency. Although I didn't realize it at the time, CNN anchor Anderson Cooper was there. He must have loved my act because a couple

Karl Giant

of days later CNN reached out to my manager about featuring me in an online piece about what it was like to be a little person in the entertainment industry. I'd done a lot of local press before, but I'd never anything on the level of CNN, so this was a huge opportunity. I gave them my schedule and they decided to send out a freelance videographer to a job Tonya and I were doing at a nightclub in Houston that October.

Beyond CNN coming out to film us, this event had special significance for Tonya because Kerwin, her on-again-off-again boyfriend and baby daddy, was living in Houston and she also had friends and family coming out to the show. It was a huge nightclub and we were the headlining for a bunch of different variety acts. Compared to some places I had worked (like the club where my "greenroom" was the handicapped stall in the lady's room) this place treated us like royalty. They had even gone out and bought us a full-length mirror because they didn't have one in the dressing room.

Just before the show, the emcee for the night came backstage to ask us how we wanted to be introduced. She was this super tall drag queen, whom I'll call Death Drop because she was known for doing a dramatic drop into a split on stage. She was at least 6 ft. 5 in. in heels—with her big hair, it was probably closer to 7 ft. 5 in. We told her our real names, that we lived in California, but we were both originally from Texas. When Death Drop left our dressing room, we figured she'd introduce us as "former Texas girls come home" or something like that. Pretty straightforward, right? Not so much.

As Tonya and I were standing in the wings waiting to take the stage, Death Drop came out to introduce us. When she took the mic, instead of introducing us the way we had discussed, we heard her say to the audience: "Who here wants to fuck a *midget*? 'Cause I got two *midgets* backstage who *love* to fuck." As Tonya and I stood there with our mouths hanging open, we heard cheers and laughter from the crowd.

Oh, hell no!

There was no way I was going out there to perform after that. Within minutes the manager of the club, who hadn't heard the offensive introduction, came backstage wanting to know why our music was playing but his headliners weren't out there performing. When we told him what had happened, he was apologetic and explained that he had called a staff meeting in advance of the night to discuss the guidelines in our contract and to ensure that everyone would be on their best behavior. Because he knew that CNN would be there, he had made sure that every employee working that night, from the bouncers to the bartenders, knew not to use this kind of offensive language. Apparently, Death Drop, who had been hired just for that event (and therefore wasn't technically "staff") never got the memo, which was unfortunate because the job of the emcee is to guide the audience and set the tone for the night. I was furious.

"No way in hell am I going out there," I told the manager. "Y'all are tripping." CNN or no CNN, I was ready to walk.

The really shameful thing is that this wasn't the first (or even the second) time something like this had happened to me—although it was by far the most offensive. Years of working as a little person in the entertainment industry taught me that I *needed* to have a clause in my contract to protect me from exactly this kind of situation. If a venue promoted me using the M-word (or any degrading language regarding my stature, my contract stipulated that I didn't have to perform *and* the venue would still have to pay me. At least twice before, I'd actually been in a car on my way to a performance when I heard some plug on the radio from the venue promoting me as "Midget Britney." Every time, I turned right around and went home and because of my contract, the venues had to pay me anyway. I *always* want to perform, but only if the environment I'm working in is safe and respectful. My contracts assure that it is the responsibility of the club or venue that hired me to make sure that happened. It was never about the money; it was about respect and taking a stand against hate speech. The sad reality for little people is that, for the most part, even within socially progressive circles it is still acceptable to ridicule us with dehumanizing language—it's one of the last forms of socially acceptable bigotry and ignorance. For all the progress that we have made as a society, there's still a fundamental lack of awareness of our struggle for equality.

The CNN videographer had been backstage when we were being introduced so he had no idea what had happened or why I was screaming at the manager of the club. When Tonya and I filled him in on what had gone down, he was sympathetic but he also had a job to do.

"Look," he said, "I get it, but in order for me to get paid, you have to go on."

"All these people are here for us," Tonya reasoned. "CNN is here. We should just hold our heads up high and not let one asshole ruin the night."

I knew this night was important to Tonya and that she wanted to avoid making any more of a scene in front of her friends and family, so I backed down and agreed to go on, but only on the condition that Death Drop go back onstage and make an official apology for what she had said. I wanted the audience to know that the language she used wasn't okay. When I came out on onto the stage, I also said a few words about ignorant people using ignorant language, and then it was right into "Just Dance." I'm sure it was a little more drama than the audience at the club that night had bargained for, but I think Lady Gaga herself would have respected my decision for taking a stand. As for Death Drop, I doubt she ever worked at that club again.

||||||||||||||||||||

MOST LP PERFORMERS HAVE A line they won't cross. For some, like me, that line is the kind of language that's used to promote us, for others there are specific roles or costume work (like leprechauns or elves) that they won't do. I've read that Peter Dinklage (probably the most famous LP actor working right now) regularly turned down character roles that he felt were demeaning to little people when he was still a struggling unknown, and I have so much respect for him for taking that stand. The problem is, there are not a lot of roles written for little people beyond the stereotypical character roles. And because there are so many of us in the industry, most of the

Egan O'Keefe

time it ends up being quantity over quality. More often than not, you're being hired to fill a costume.

As a performer, I have put up with a lot of ignorance because people don't always get that you are practicing a craft. They think anybody can throw on a blonde wig and dance around the stage like Lady Gaga or Britney, but the show that I put on (from the costumes to the choreography) was a polished performance and that was reflected in the fact that I was in such demand. I was even on an episode of *CSI: Las Vegas*, as Mini Britney, where I recorded my own vocals. It was an empowering experience because they took me seriously as a performer and treated me with respect. Jobs like that made all the other crap I put up with worthwhile.

Even within the LP community there's a lot of controversy surrounding the work we do as performers. A lot of little people have strong feelings about impersonation work in particular because they feel it's demeaning. In my opinion, it's the opposite because *you* are in control. If you let them laugh *at* you they will, but the sign of a strong performer is when you are in command of the crowd and you have them laughing *with* you. I've faced a lot of criticism over the years, but I have no regrets about the choices I've made in my career. Every time I took the stage as a character, whether it was for Radio City or as Mini Britney, I viewed it as an acting role and a chance to hone my craft.

CHAPTER TWELVE

LITTLE LADIES

After Joe and I split up, he went off to do *Mirror Mirror* with Julia Roberts in Canada, which totally turned things around for him. He was doing really well in his career and was in a much different place than he had been a year and a half earlier. When you're working, you're happy because you're not jumping from job to job and living paycheck to paycheck. Joe was getting on with his life and dating an average-sized woman in Canada, but he never gave up on us. Every few days he would call or send me a text. At first, I'd respond maybe every couple of weeks, but he just kept reaching out, and eventually we sort of innocently fell into a routine of talking regularly.

In the time that we were apart, I had a few flings. The infatuation would last a couple weeks, or even a month or two, but I never had that butterflies feeling I had with Joe. Even though I was getting out and dating like a hooker, deep down I wasn't happy without Joe in my life. Not only did we have a strong physical attraction, Joe could make me cry with laughter. Nobody that I ever dated could make me laugh like that. Once we started talking again, we would have these long conversations about anything and everything. Then one day we both just realized that we were still very much in love and we were finally ready to be together again. We had given each other the time and space we each needed to see what else was out there, which neither of us had really experienced before, and we were stronger as a couple for it. Joe was still living in our apartment in Fullerton, but I knew we needed to leave all our old baggage behind, so we decided to move into a new place in Roland Heights and start fresh.

|||||||||||||||||||||||

MEANWHILE, I WAS STILL SEARCHING for my purpose as a performer. I felt as if I had reached the peak of what I could accomplish touring as Mini Britney and Mini Gaga, and it was time to move forward. Tonya felt the same way, and one day we sat down together to talk about what was next for us. Ever since the *Four Foot Two* show had fallen through, I couldn't get it out of my head that we should come up with a new original show that was based on us. Female-driven reality shows in the spirit of *Real Housewives* and *Basketball Wives* were huge at the time, so I said to Tonya, "What if we do that type of show, but with little people." Tonya thought it was a great idea, so I said, "Great. I'll organize everything." At the time, my idea was to shoot a series of 8-minute online episodes. It seemed like something I could produce relatively cheaply, and then put them out there to see how people reacted. I told Tonya we should call the series *Little Ladies: LA.*

"Why not just *Little Ladies*?" was her reaction.

"No. It has to be *Little Ladies: LA*," I insisted. "That way if the show is successful, it leaves us open to the possibility of doing shows with Little Ladies in other cities."

I could already see the hashtags: #LLLA, #LLATL, #LLNY. I wanted to secure my idea, so I registered *Little Ladies: LA* with the Writer's Guild of America.

I wanted our concept to be unique in that all the women on the show would already have real history and real relationships with one another. So I started thinking about all the little ladies I knew in Los Angeles to come up with the perfect blend of characters. I remember sitting for hours at a glass table on the patio in my backyard with a notebook, writing down everything I knew about each of the girls I was considering; I even kept detailed notes on a list of alternates. Every single one of the ladies I picked for the show that first season was selected for a very specific reason.

Tonya was obviously at the top of my list, not just because she is my one of my best friends and we love working together, but because she is such a talented, smart, strong-minded, and hilarious individual. She has no filter and strong opinions, and I knew viewers would fall in love with her. The next person I brought in was Traci. She was one of the first people I had met when I first moved out to California and we bonded instantly; she was actually in my episode of *True Life*. Even though she wasn't a performer, Traci had gotten her license to be an on-set teacher so she knew a lot of LPs in the entertainment industry and was very entwined with all the other women I was considering for the show. Because she comes from a very affluent, conservative, religious background I also knew she would make an interesting contrast to the rest of us. We met for lunch at her parents' country club, and when I pitched her my idea for the show she he loved it and was totally game.

I met Christy through my roommate Amy (who by then was living in Arizona, so she wasn't able to be a part of the show

Traci (middle) and I with Amy (far right), shortly after I moved to LA.

herself) when I first moved out to LA. I thought she'd be a great fit for the show because she had worked in the industry as a dancer and an actress and had known Traci and Tonya for years. I knew Briana peripherally through her ex-husband, whom I had known since we were teenagers. We never worked together before and she wasn't really on my radar, but it just so happened that around this time she, Tonya, and I were cast as members of a LP gospel choir in a comedy music video. I remember the three of us were driving to the gig together, and

131

Briana was talking about all of her problems at home and how she was going through a divorce. I hadn't initially thought of her for the show, but listening to how complicated her life was and how she was so open about all of it, I kept thinking that she had such a great emotional storyline that a lot of people could relate to her.

Tonya was driving and Briana was sitting next to her in the front seat, so I leaned forward and said, "Tonya, what do you think of Briana for the show?" We told Briana about it and she was totally game. I didn't know a ton about her, but I felt if she could be that open with two people she barely knew, she would probably be as honest on camera. Plus, she was so drastically different from the rest of us visually, and I really wanted to represent all little people.

Elena was the easiest and fastest "yes" of the group. I knew nothing about her other than she came from Russia and was married to an average-sized man; she could be totally boring but she was so gorgeous I figured we could make it work. I only knew her to say hi or make small talk at auditions, so I decided to call her to get a better sense of who she was. I was surprised by how normal she was. I've met so many crazy characters in the LP community that it was refreshing to talk to someone who seemed so confident and grounded. I really admired those qualities in her, and I felt like the rest of the women, myself included, were all so out there that maybe she would be a calming influence. If nothing else, at the time she was doing her version of Mini Gaga at the Roosevelt, so I figured that alone might at least provide an interesting energy between us.

Of all of us, Elena was the only one who didn't know what kind of dwarfism she had. I remember thinking she could have pituitary dwarfism or cartilage-hair hypoplasia (Jasmine's kind

of dwarfism) because her body is so proportionate, but she didn't have the brittle hair that is a characteristic of cartilage-hairs and she had also complained about having hip issues, which would have been unusual for a pituitary. The first time she took her shoes off I knew for sure she was pseudo; her feet looked just like Joe's (minus the hair). I told her, "Those are pseudo feet." She thought I was crazy to diagnosis her dwarfism by her feet, but when she finally had the testing done it turned out I was right.

|||||||||||||||||||||

AT THIS POINT THERE WAS no deal, so the girls all agreed to do the project for free in the hope that once we got our concept off the ground we would get network interest and contracts for all of us to do the show. Tonya's fiftieth birthday was coming up in a few weeks so we decided to invite the core six ladies, film the party, and make a pilot out of it. Then, out of the blue, I got a call from Kinetic Content, a production company based in Los Angeles, that was looking to cast a reality show with a small group of little people girlfriends. I told them I was working on a similar project but that I was interested in hearing more about their concept.

Kinetic had done *The Taste* on ABC and *Betty White's Off Their Rockers*, a hidden camera show featuring Betty White (obviously), on NBC. I was impressed that Kinetic was network connected, but I also knew that the big networks tend to be more interested in competition-based reality TV shows. Given that our show would be about six strong women, I loved that Kinetic is a very female-driven company; I felt like they would allow me a lot of creative input. I knew the idea we had been conceptualizing had the potential to be a hit, so when I met with Kinetic's team, I was determined to make my pitch as professional as possible. I went in there armed with detailed spreadsheets, with photos, and bullet points highlighting each of the girls' backgrounds and characters. They loved my concept and asked if they could send someone from casting to Tonya's birthday to check us out and to see what we were all about.

Even though I was very confident in our concept, what we were doing was truly raw, guerrilla filmmaking. I knew there was no way that I could achieve the production value Kinetic was capable of, but I still wanted to shoot our own episode to see what I could come up with. At Tonya's fiftieth birthday party, I went around with my little Cannon 7D, and filmed all the girls interacting with one another. (The interviews ended up being the most interesting footage because all the girls were so willing to talk shit about each other on camera.) I edited the footage into an 8-minute teaser and, while it wasn't perfect, for a first shot I was impressed with what I was able to pull together. I *knew* we had something special on our hands. I brought the footage to the higher-ups at Kinetic and they loved it. They believed in the potential of my idea, and asked how I felt about collaborating and creating something together. It was such a no-brainer for us to move forward with Kinetic because I truly believed in their vision and I knew they would collaborate with me. I felt like it was meant to be, and I haven't looked back since.

After we signed the deal, they had a big production meeting and decided to change the name of our show to *Little Women: L.A.* As much as I liked my title, I was okay with the change because I felt like they were more equipped to make that call than I was. Kinetic also wanted to film their own teaser, so they had the six of us get together at a Greek diner in Brentwood. The energy that night was easy and organic and I knew in my heart of hearts that we had a hit on our hands. The only question was whether Kinetic would be able to sell it to a network.

CHAPTER THIRTEEN

THE END OF THE RAINBOW

After we filmed in Brentwood, Kinetic took the pilot to New York to pitch the show to various cable and network television companies. At that point, it was out of our hands. We figured it would be months before we heard anything, so we were all shocked when we got the call from Kinetic just a few days later that they already had interest from a couple of networks. They must have liked what they saw in the teaser, because now they wanted to meet all six of us in person to get a sense of our individual personalities and if the dynamic between us was real.

Within days we found ourselves gathered in a boardroom to meet with network executives. I doubt it would surprise anyone that the six of us ended up getting into a huge argument right in the middle the meeting. How it went down was this: someone made a comment about the M-word being just as offensive as the N-word, which triggered Tonya (who totally disagreed). Next thing you know, all six of us were talking and shouting over one another, expressing our very strong opinions and taking sides in the debate. It got pretty heated. I remember at one point one of the executives even made a comment that it was too bad they weren't filming. When we walked out of that meeting, some of the girls were convinced we had blown our big opportunity, but I was like, "Are you kidding? Y'all, we just gave them gold." A few weeks later we were told that there were six different networks vying for the show, and sure enough those same executives were among the bidders.

At that point, even though we had a lot of interest in the show, Kinetic let us know that it was still going to be a long haul, so we told them that we were looking forward to running this race with them and reaching the finish line together, and then we all went back to pursuing our own projects. After the experience of having a pilot fall through, I was much more cautious about getting my hopes up this time. I decided to sign on to do Radio City in New York that Christmas season, so that no matter what happened with the pilot I knew I would have health insurance locked down for the year.

Meanwhile, that August, Miley Cyrus's production company contacted me; they were looking for little people to perform with her at the 2013 Video Music Awards at the Barclays Center in New York. I had passed because I already had way too much on my plate, but I referred them to a few LP dancers I knew in the area. Little did I know that Miley's performance that night was going blow up in such a big way.

A week later, I was sitting on my back patio when my cell phone rang. It was Miley's people again. This time they were looking to put together a band that they could take on tour and they wanted LPs who could actually play instruments. Because I was so well connected in the LP community, it wasn't unusual for production companies to contact me when they had specific roles they were looking to fill. I told them about Joe, and sent them a video of him playing the drums. Within twenty minutes, they called back wanting to know if Joe had a passport. Two days later he was on a flight to Europe for a three-city press tour of Cologne, Paris, and London. Truth be told, I tried to pitch myself for the tour as well, but at that point they were only looking for male LPs.

A day or two after Joe came back from Europe, Miley's people reached out again. This time they wanted help putting together some dancers for a few dates leading up her big US/European Bangerz Tour, which was to kick off in early 2014. I reached out to every LP dancer I knew in LA and asked them to send me audition tapes. I sent her people about ten videos, including my own. Tonya even came over to my house so I could help her put together a tape; we still had no idea if the show with Kinetic would happen and touring with Miley was a huge opportunity. All my life, I have always had long blonde hair that fell down to my lower back, but when we had started filming the pilot in July I wanted to have a different look from Elena. So, I cut my hair short and shaved the sides—and it just so happened that my new look was similar to Miley's at the time.

After Miley's production company's initial reaction to my audition tape (which was basically, "Sorry, but we're going in a different direction"), I was definitely not feeling good about my chances. But a few minutes later they called me back to say Miley wanted me and Jordanna James (who would later become a cast member on the first season of *Little Women: NY*), so now they were only looking for one more dancer. I already knew Jordanna through Radio City, so I was psyched to be working with her again. Jordanna has great energy; she has one of those personalities that everyone likes. She is an incredibly talented dancer and had been working with Radio City New York since she was a teenager. There are only a few children in the cast, and those are almost always average-sized dancers, so the fact that when they hired Jordanna they'd also hired an on-set tutor to keep up with school is an indication of just how talented a dancer she is.

A week later, Miley's production company held a physical audition for about twenty LP dancers to fill the last remaining spot on the tour. First, they had all the dancers freestyle; you could tell who Miley enjoyed because she would jump in and dance alongside them. At one point, they had all the dancers in a circle and then each one would come to the center do a little freestyle and then go back out. Towards the end, they started telling people to go to the side of the circle, until the only two dancers left were Brittney Guzman (who would later join us for one season of *Little Women: LA*) and her father, David. They are both really talented dancers, and you can tell Brittney gets her skills from her dad. I'd known Brittney and her parents for years. In fact, when I first moved out to LA in 2001, we all went to an LPA Halloween party together. She was about ten or eleven at the time and she was in costume as Josie from *Josie and The Pussycats*, and Traci and I decided it would be fun to go as her Pussycats.

After the audition, Jordanna and I went straight into rehearsal. In the morning, we were joined by Brittney who had snagged the final dancer spot. Other than Jordanna, who was the featured dancer, all the dancers (LP and average-sized) were going to be in costumes with limited use of our arms, so it was a lot of lower body movement and swaying. The choreography was pretty much like this: step, step, sway; twerk, march, march; step, step sway; twerk, march. We had a couple of weeks of rehearsals and by the end of September we were off to Las

Vegas to perform in two back-to-back concerts for I Heart Radio. Miley's set was very bright and colorful, like Super Mario Brothers on 'shrooms. Most of the dancers were dressed as mushrooms and flowers; there was even a two-person rainbow costume. It was all very trippy and bright. I've done all kinds of costume work, but dressing up as a psychedelic mushroom was definitely a first for me.

What I loved about working with Miley is how incredibly warm and inviting she is. Not only is she an absolute professional, she is totally down to earth. Even though she is truly a megastar, and has been since the age of eleven, she doesn't have an attitude that she's better than anyone. You can always tell when you meet someone for the first time if they've been around little people before. With Miley, you can tell that she is used to being around little people from her days when she was a child star and LPs stood-in for her on set. She's very comfortable with little people because she's been around us all her life, and while on tour with her we were treated with nothing but respect.

However, not every little person who has worked with Miley sees it that way. By the time we got to New York, after the I Heart Radio shows, it was all over the news that one of the backup dancers who'd been in her now-infamous VMA performance had come out with a scathing attack on Miley. She claimed that she had felt exploited and that the experience made her feel ashamed of being little for the first time in her life. On the morning of our live broadcast on *Today*, Miley sat down with Brittney, Jordanna, and I to ask how we felt about what had been said. We assured her that we were all baffled by the attack because it was so far from what we were experiencing.

While I totally respect anyone's right to express an opinion and to put forward a strong voice for LP performers, *my* experience working with Miley was one of the most positive of my career. We felt empowered because Miley has a love and appreciation for people of all shapes and sizes. It felt like we were all in it together. So, in response to any criticism and speculation in the media that Miley was exploiting the little people on her tour, she tweeted a pic of us sitting on the couch braiding one another's hair, along with the tag: #aslongasmybitchesloveme.

IIIIIIIIIIIIIIIIIII

I SHOULD HAVE BEEN THE happiest I'd ever been. My baby (the show) was gaining traction with some networks, I was about to perform with Miley Cyrus on the *Today* show, I had Radio City New York lined up for the Christmas season, and I was in a loving, happy relationship with Joe. Both my personal life and my career were at an all-time high, but it was also the saddest period of my life because my father, who had been diagnosed with cirrhosis of the liver in 2011, was in the hospital again; this time, for his second liver transplant.

I found out he was going into the hospital again just after we left for I Heart Radio. As much as I wanted to be with him, my dad insisted that I stay on the tour. More than anyone else in my life, my dad loved the fact that I was making a career as a performer. He understood where my passion came from, and he made me feel like I could do anything. Dad knew all about Miley and would brag to all the doctors and nurses in the hospital that his daughter was going to be on *Today* with Hannah Montana.

The first time he told us that he was going to need a transplant, my dad was very nonchalant about it. It wasn't like he ever sat us down to explain it all; he just dropped it into a conversation one day: "So, I'm on the waiting list for a liver transplant." He made it seem like he was going in for a teeth

Me and Dad, riding a lawn-mower at the Big House in Canyon Lake.

cleaning. The longest I could ever keep him on the phone was about five minutes, so whatever information I got about his health was condensed into that amount of time. I don't know if it was hard for him to open up or if he just didn't want us to see him be vulnerable. I don't think he was trying to keep it from us, but he was definitely downplaying how serious it all was. He was still the guy who wasn't going to stop cooking or entertaining. He didn't want life to stop just because he was sick.

For years, his doctor had been telling him to quit drinking, but he never took it seriously enough. Being put on the transplant list scared the shit out of him. It was stop drinking or die, because he was at the point where his health was deteriorating so quickly that it wouldn't be long before he wasn't a viable candidate for a transplant anymore. As far as I could tell, right before the first transplant he did finally quit drinking, but by then he was already very sick. The waiting list was about eighty names long, and he started off in the middle of the list. Then he jumped to the twenties, and then to the top ten. The lower you are the on the list, the sicker you are, so by the time you get to the top five names you don't have much time left. As much as we wanted him to get a new liver, it was hard because you're basically waiting for someone to die so your father can live.

After the first transplant, he seemed to regain his health and was back to his old self. Then, three months later he started having pain in his abdomen. He went in for tests and they discovered that the liver he'd been given was infected with cancer. Very quickly after that he started losing weight again and feeling the effects of the cancer. It was worse than before. Almost immediately he looked older, thin, and frail. He had always been a hefty dude with a classic beer belly, and muscular calves (which were completely hairless because his work pants had buffed them to a shine). But after he got sick from the cancer, he lost all that fat and muscle to the point where skin was literally hanging off his body. Cancer is a demon that destroys you from the inside.

On top of living with cancer, he had to go through all the insurance and hospital approvals again, which was incredibly stressful. That took a couple of months; once he was approved he was so sick he was put right into the top ten on the waiting list. After that the waiting time could be a day or a year, you never know. He was really strong about it, but you could tell this time he was worried. His energy level was down, and you could see the fear behind his eyes. I went home every other month, and every time I saw him he was more and more a shadow of

himself. The whole time I kept thinking *everything is going to be okay*—because it was the first time—but really, it wasn't okay.

Late that September he was fast-tracked to the top five on the waiting list. Then, almost immediately, he got word they had a liver for him and he went in to the hospital for the transplant surgery. I was in Vegas and I wanted to come home, but when I called him he said, "I've been bragging to all the nurses about you. I'm fine. Go to New York. Work comes first. I'll see you after I get out of the hospital." He was so excited about the

My father, Richard Odmark,
as a young man.

Today show, that I felt like I would have let him down if I came home. The surgery went well and they kept him for extra tests this time, so we were all very optimistic he was going to be okay. My plan was to do the *Today* show on October 7 and then fly back to San Antonio that night. On October 3, the day he was to be released, my dad suffered a massive heart attack and died in the hospital. He never made it home. He never got to see me perform. And I never got to say goodbye.

For a long time after that, I had a hard time processing my emotions because I never really had any closure. My biggest regret in life is that I never got to see my dad before he died to tell him how much I loved him, and how much his support meant to me all these years. I still live with that sadness and anger that he had to endure a second surgery when his heart wasn't strong enough, plus the guilt of not being there by his side when he died.

||||||||||||||||||||

FOUR DAYS AFTER MY DAD died, I performed on *Today* with Miley and that night I flew home to be with my family. I needed closure, but there was no funeral or memorial. He was just gone. The only thing I had wanted of his was a black box of index cards where he kept all his recipes, but by time got back to San Antonio my stepmother had thrown them out. I was heartbroken.

I was home for five days and then I flew back to New York to do Radio City, but I was a mess. In rehearsals I'd be fine one minute and then a wave of grief would wash over me, and I'd break down. I was living in a rough neighborhood in Harlem and rooming with a cast member from the show. We had opposite schedules, so I'd leave early in the morning and work all day and she would leave in the afternoon and come home late at night. It was a very lonely time. At one point, somebody was stabbed in broad daylight right across the street from our building. I remember coming home exhausted after a show the next day and there was still blood all over the sidewalk. All I could think was, "Isn't anybody going to clean that up?" That was definitely a low point.

Then, at the end of October, I got *the* call from Kinetic: Hold on to your seat; we sold the show and we're going with Lifetime. Instead of excitement, I remember feeling stressed because not only was I under contract with Radio City until the end of the year, I was supposed to be going on tour in January, which would have been a year-long commitment. I held off telling Miley's people as long as possible because there was a big part of me that felt like, they're talking a big game right now, but I'll believe it when cameras are up.

Once all the paperwork was signed, and it was official that we were to begin filming *Little Women: LA* in January, there was no turning back. I called Miley's people and told them that, unfortunately, I couldn't be part of the tour. The last thing I wanted to do was let anyone down, but I was at a crossroads and I felt like if there was a chance this show would help me get my own name out there, then I had to take it.

When we started filming I went into it feeling very cautious. I had been down this road before and I knew how easily things can fall apart. In some ways, it was a very carefree moment because I had no idea what was going to happen and no expectations. I just took this leap that if it was meant to be, it would work out. It wasn't until mid-March, when we got together to film the opener for the show that it started to seem real. They were filming at this jazz-age Parisian-style cocktail lounge on Melrose called Pour Vous, and I remember thinking the whole thing felt so glam. There was a makeup trailer and craft services; Lifetime had spared no expense. Executives were telling us they believed in the show and that we were part of the Lifetime family. I remember looking at Tonya and realizing for the first time: *This is real*.

The best part was that Tonya and I were there together. We had been friends through Radio City and Little Legends, through Mini Britney and Mini Beyoncé, and now we were on a new journey together. And the craziest part of the whole experience was the fact that it was created out of nothing and we turned it into a career.

|||||||||||||||||||||

THE FIRST EPISODE OF *Little Women: LA* debuted on May 27, 2014, two days after my thirty-fourth birthday. At the premier party, we had a cake for my birthday and watched the episode on huge screens around the bar. Nobody knew what to expect, but we came out of the gate strong; by the fourth episode we were reaching over a million viewers. From that moment on our lives were never the same.

It is one thing to be on tour, performing in front of thousands of people, but the show catapulted us to a whole new level of celebrity that nothing could have prepared me for. It was a surreal transition for all of us; we were used to people staring at us on the street, but suddenly it wasn't because we were "little" but because they recognized us from the show. Before *Little Women LA*, we'd all had experiences of some random person taking a photo because they'd never seen a little person before, or because they wanted to amuse their friends. It was upsetting because it felt like a violation. Then, literally overnight, people were taking photos of us because they were fans. That was mind-blowing. On the other hand, although it was a thrill to have a show, it was more about my personal life than about me as a performer, and that took a lot of getting used to. For so long I had wanted to take the next step in my career and to be out front as Terra Jolé, but this wasn't necessarily the way I had always envisioned it would happen. Be careful what you wish for, I guess.

One of the hardest things about watching the show that first season was how driven it was by our fights. Going in, we thought it was going to be a show about six friends, but at times it can seem more like a show about six frenemies. I don't think any of us had any idea that the friction between us would become such a feature of the show. We all have such strong personalities and I knew there would be conflict (I was counting on it), but I guess I had always thought the arguments would be entertaining, but not necessarily the focus.

As amazing as it was that the show was doing so well, there was also something very scary about having your personal life become so public. Suddenly, people I didn't know were dissecting my relationship with Joe and judging us on what they saw on the show. During the first season, you're never ready for any negative comments. Joe and I would be out to dinner or at the grocery store and total strangers would come up to us to make comments like, "Joe, you need to treat her better." Internet trolls would send us nasty tweets or post hateful comments on Facebook. Joe felt like he was being cast as the villain and it was rough on him. When people started describing our house and making actual threats to Joe like, "You're going to pay for how you treated Terra," that's when we reached out to the police—I never knew until I was in the limelight that the Los Angeles County Police maintains a special department to handle threats against celebrities.

It was a much harder transition for Joe. He agreed to do the show because he loves me and knew it was something *I* really wanted, but he came from an acting background and was not a fan of reality television. I don't think he's ever regretted it, but there definitely have been moments where he felt like this wasn't what he signed up for. It can be really hard not to react to negative comments, and it takes a tremendous amount of restraint not to explode back on haters.

CHAPTER FOURTEEN

PENNY FROM HEAVEN

When I found out I was pregnant, I was definitely scared. I had always wanted a big family and Joe and I had talked about having children (someday), but this wasn't something we had planned. I was worried that we weren't ready, that this wasn't the right time for us, and that people were going to judge us for not being married. During Season 1 so many of the girls were at a point in their lives where they were ready to have children, so when we came back for Season 2, I was thinking everyone's going to be popping up pregnant. Never in a million years did I think it would be *me* as the one making the big announcement.

At that point in my life, having a baby could not have been further from my mind, but once it happened it just felt right. Joe and I were living together in Roland Heights; we'd talked about getting married and we were definitely in a good place, but we weren't necessarily prepared for parenthood. At first Joe was just in disbelief, but almost immediately his energy shifted to excitement. It definitely took a minute for us to wrap our minds around the fact that we were about to become parents,

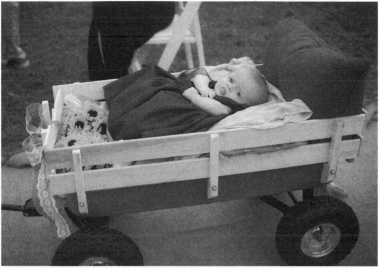

Jason Brown

but once we did, we felt nothing but joy. Knowing we had created a life together anchored our relationship and took away all the doubt and searching.

Honestly, I was more scared to tell my mom than anyone else that I was pregnant. It wasn't that I didn't think she would be supportive; it was more that I didn't want her to be disappointed in me. She has never understood the life I've chosen for myself, the uncertainty of living paycheck to paycheck. That's how my life has been the last seventeen-plus years, and she gets scared for me because it isn't always easy. My mom always wanted me to follow a path similar to that of my brother. He still lives in San Antonio and for more than a decade he's had the same, steady job as the manager of the accounting department of a local grocery store. She still feels like if it were up to her, I'd be back in San Antonio, working a 9 to 5 with a steady salary, health insurance, and a 401K.

When we told her about the baby, there was a part of me that felt like a little girl again. I needed her approval and for her to be proud of me. Comparing the timelines of our lives, my mother and I have so much overlap. I was having a child at the same age that she had me; Joe and I had been together as long as she had been with my dad when they had kids; and my career was as stable as it had ever been. But, she just couldn't see it that way. At the time, I couldn't understand why she couldn't just be happy for us, but now that I have kids of my own I get it. Her biggest concern was my health; she was petrified of what the pregnancy would do to my body. I have a couple of achon friends who have permanent disabilities because of the additional weight that their pregnancies put on their spines.

There's no way to predict what having a baby will do to your body; it's such an unknown and this terrified my mom. This was around the same time that my godmother Betty was having debilitating back and hip issues; her health was deteriorating in large part due to the strain being overweight put on her body and the surgeries required to correct the damage. Betty died of a stroke in January 2016. She spent the last years of her life bedridden and in agonizing pain after enduring a hip replacement procedure, followed almost immediately by a painful spinal fusion surgery. With little people, our spinal cords are average size, but the bones don't develop so it causes the spine to compress. It's very common for LPs with achondroplasia to have this spinal fusion procedure, but Betty should never have had the two surgeries so closely together. I personally blame her diminishing health on doctors who understood very little about little people. My mom was watching her best friend suffer, and the last thing she wanted was to see her daughter go through all of that. She has always wanted to protect me from the health risks that come along with achondroplasia, and because she can't it makes her feel helpless.

Bourn, on the other hand, was onboard from the second we told him. He's always been great with kids. I think my brother could have children and no wife and be totally happy. He's still single and has that strong boy mentality, which makes him the ultimate uncle. He has always been such a stable and calming force in our family, and I think seeing how excited he was about my baby coming into the world put all of us at ease.

|||||||||||||||||||||||

WE KNEW FROM THE ULTRASOUNDS that we were having a girl, but I could also tell that she was achon like me. Not only was her head developing proportionately larger, the ultrasound technicians had captured one image where we could clearly see the palm of her hand, like she was holding it up to the screen, and she had our characteristic curving in her fingers. Because I had minimal health issues related to my achondroplasia, I had just assumed my baby would be healthy too. We could see in the sonogram that she had clubbing in her feet (like I had), but we also knew that it would resolve itself in time. I was prepared for health issues related to bone growth, but I was *not* prepared for my doctor telling me at seven months that he was concerned she might have hydrocephalus, a condition where fluid begins to build up and put harmful pressure on the brain. The only way to know for sure was to have an MRI so they could do a more detailed scan of her brain. Terrified does not begin to convey the free-fall of fear you experience as an expecting mother when you get news like this about your unborn child.

Meanwhile, after we wrapped Season 2 of *Little Women: LA*, the network approached me about doing a two- to four-episode special that would focus on my pregnancy and delivery. At that point, I was about eight months pregnant and, between having an MIR while my baby was in the womb and the possibility that my child may have hydrocephalus, I was so wracked with anxiety that the last thing I was thinking about was having my own show. I was a bit wary making that part of our lives so public, but I figured if we could give people an insight into some of the difficulties little people face during pregnancy, or help even one person who was going through something similar, then it would be worth it.

At the beginning of my ninth month, I went in for the MRI. You have to lie there perfectly still inside this tunnel-like machine for an hour and a half. The sound the MRI machine makes is like the loudest fax machine you've ever heard, so they give you headphones and a list of movie options to keep you occupied. Once I was inside the machine, a voice came through the speaker: "We're going to start the movie now. Don't press the red button unless you're in pain." I'll never forget, instead of the 007 movie I had picked out and was all settled in to watch, the movie that came on was *The Sisterhood of the Traveling Pants 2*. I was like, *Really? Can I push the red button now?*

The MRI confirmed what we already feared: our baby had a dangerous buildup of fluid putting pressure on her brain. If left untreated, she would be at risk of permanent brain damage. We were told that there was a chance it might resolve itself, but most likely she would eventually have to have a drainage tube, called a shunt, surgically inserted into the base of her skull down through the chest cavity to drain the fluid from her brain. Even though we knew this surgery might be necessary, it comes with its own health risks. The shunt can malfunction or clog, which can cause seizures and strokes that lead to permanent brain damage. Even if nothing goes wrong, the worst part was that as a baby she would outgrow the shunt every few years and then she would have to have the surgery again.

When the big day came for my C-section, all I wanted was to hold my baby in my arms; that's all any mother wants. When a healthy baby comes into the world, you hear them wailing as their tiny little lungs fill with air for the first time. When Penelope was born, she didn't make a sound. The silence of those first few moments, as the doctor and nurses pumped the fluid from her lungs and gave her oxygen to help her breath, seemed to last forever.

Once she was stabilized, Penelope Charlevoix Gnoffo was whisked off to the NICU and I was taken to a recovery room. I never got to hold her. I didn't even get to see her until the next day. I had caught a glimpse of Joe through the curtains of the NICU as they wheeled me to the recovery room, but that was it. Because of the anesthesia they gave me for the C-section, I still couldn't walk the next day so they put me in a chair and wheeled me to the NICU. When the nurses pulled the curtain back so I could see my daughter for the first time, it was love at first sight. There are no words to describe the mixture of joy and sadness to look at your child for the very first time, but not be able to hold or even touch her.

During all of that insanity, they were filming for the special. It was one camera guy and the executive producer of the show, Eric. Through all of it, Eric was amazing. He brought such a positive energy to the experience and because he made me feel so at ease I was able to share one of the most intimate and intense moments of my life. The day after Penelope was born, Eric came to see me with some big news. Admittedly, I was on a lot of pain mediation from the C-section, but I was really having a hard time processing what he was trying to tell me. Apparently, Lifetime wanted to expand the special into a full show called *Terra's Little Family* and they had just bought another twenty-four episodes extended over two seasons.

It felt like I was at the center of a hurricane. There was so much happening around me—a new baby, a new show, the uncertainty and fear surrounding my child's health—I could barely catch my breath, much less make sense of it all. It was insanity how something that was so totally unexpected became so much bigger than I ever imagined. To this day, the episode of *Terra's Little Family* where I gave birth to Penelope has the highest ratings of any other episode of all the *Little Women* franchises.

||||||||||||||||||||

IT'S CRAZY HOW, ONCE YOU have children, it's not exactly that you can't remember your life before, it's more that you can't imagine *how* you ever lived without them. Penny changed everything. Once this beautiful child came into our lives, our relationship felt fuller and stronger than ever. In those early months, Joe and I would be up in the middle of the night multiple times to feed her; we'd be deliriously tired but he'd stop me on the way to get her bottle or a fresh diaper and just kiss me.

Children can make or break a marriage, and in our case, it made us stronger. It became a blessing for us, because it tested the bonds of our relationship and we learned just how strong we really were. Joe was there for me through every step of the pregnancy. He came to every doctor's appointment (and towards the end I was going two or three times a week). By that point I was so huge I couldn't fit behind the wheel of our car, so he would drive me everywhere. When Penelope was born, he was so dedicated. I never had to ask him for anything; he just stepped up and was the perfect dad and loving partner. I used to tease him that he loved his cat more than me, and with Penelope I saw that same kind of devotion and unconditional love.

About a month before Penny was born, Joe took me on a helicopter ride—which right away should have been a red flag because he is not a fan of heights. We were filming for the special, so I just assumed it was another crazy show excursion. I was so close to giving birth I was ready to pop and I wasn't really supposed to be flying, but Joe had gotten approval from my doctor. I was psyched to see what the day had in store for us. We were given a full tour through downtown LA on the helicopter ride and for the first few minutes after we took off Joe was smiling like, "This is so amazing." Then almost immediately he started getting nauseous and I just kept telling him to look at the horizon. Kinetic wanted to get aerial shots so we were flying low, zooming in and out of buildings on either side of us. I love roller coasters, but even I was terrified on this flight.

We landed on a hill overlooking the ocean in Malibu, where a picnic was set up for us. When Joe started talking about his feelings I knew something was up because he's just not that kind of guy. He has a hard time expressing himself when it comes to how he feels in an intimate relationship. He had been very secretive the whole day and now I knew why. When he proposed, it was so romantic and so beautiful. I knew I was ready to spend forever with this man. Joe was, and still is, the love of my life.

We got married on Father's Day, three months after Penny was born, in Oswego, Illinois. I had always wanted a wedding by the water, someplace that reminded me of growing up in

Canyon Lake. We found this farm with a beautiful country field, beside a tranquil little pond. As a surprise for Joe I had arranged for an acoustic instrumentation of "1979" to play as I walked down the aisle. It was everything I could ask for. The one wrinkle was that it was incredibly hot and the ground was muddy from rain the day before. As I made my way down the aisle my heel broke off. All I wanted to do was stop and chuck my shoes off, but I didn't want to ruin the moment.

Until I met Joe, I never felt that I wanted to be with any man forever. Even after we were together, for years I never felt content or satisfied enough. Maybe it's the Gemini in me (or maybe I'm a bitch) but I never felt that I was totally happy until we had Penelope. Now, for the first time in my life I was going to be bound to one man forever and it felt right. Joe and I had gone through so much with Penny's diagnosis and now we were facing her surgery. We were so new to everything: we were new to parenting, new to having a child with health issues, new to being a family. But as we stood there and said our vows before our family and dearest friends, I knew that I had found my partner in life.

|||||||||||||||||||||

WHEN PENELOPE WAS FOUR MONTHS old, we noticed that she wasn't using her arms much and whenever we put her in her car seat or tried to sit her up she would lean her head back. It's common with achons for spinal compression to put pressure on the foramen magnum, the opening where your skull connects to the spinal cord. The reason she was leaning her head back was to relieve the pain she felt whenever she had to do something where her chin was to her chest, like sitting up in a stroller or high seat, because her spine was being pinched. She was already having regular MRIs to monitor the hydrocephalus and the imaging showed she already had some damage to her spine. She would need to have a decompression surgery as soon as possible, which meant that the doctors would shave off a piece of the bone at the base of her skull to make the opening larger and relieve the pressure on her spine. It's a common surgery among achons; Traci and Tonya have had it. Surgery is always risky for little people, and it's all that much more dangerous for LP infants. But the alternative was that Penny would be paralyzed by the time she was a teenager.

They were still monitoring the hydrocephalus to see whether Penny would need to have the shunt, but in the meantime the decompression surgery became our number one priority. We actually had a surgery scheduled when Penny was four months old, but I had called every mom I could find with an achon baby who had gone through this surgery to ask how old they were when they had it. Across the board, they all said they waited until their children were seven months, so the night before the surgery I called to cancel and then found a new doctor who had much more extensive experience with little people. We are human, but we're built differently from average-sized people, so we need to have doctors who understand all the issues that come along with our physical makeup.

Before the surgery, Penny was just starting to hold her head up (late for an average-sized baby but on schedule for an LP) After the surgery, she would have to start all over again and it was difficult to see her going backward. Our doctor told us there was a slight chance that surgery could help relieve some of the pressure the fluid was putting on her brain. He had seen it happen in some cases, but there was no medical proof that the decompression surgery would help the hydrocephalus. At the time of this writing, Penny has had one surgery and five MRIs. Every time we have to put her through the experience of being sedated and poked and prodded, Joe and I can barely breathe until she is safely back in our arms. So far, we are still holding off on the shunt and overall, we've seen a vast improvement, but we are not out if the woods. We'll probably end up monitoring her for the rest of her life. But, despite all the stress and pain we have endured as parents, nothing can compare to the joy our daughter has brought to our lives.

||||||||||||||||||||||

BEING LP PARENTS MEANS THAT with every pregnancy there is a 50 percent chance our baby will be born with either my type or Joe's type of dwarfism. There's also a 25 percent chance our baby could be born with both genes, but double dominant babies rarely survive past the first few months. Just before Penny's decompression surgery, I found out I was pregnant with our second child. It was definitely a lot to take on at the time, but I knew in my heart that we could handle whatever challenge a new baby would mean for our little family.

With Penelope, I had gained half my body weight and I was definitely worried about putting that much strain on my body again. With the second pregnancy, I didn't gain as much weight,

Belly shot at 8½ months.

Our little family.

but unfortunately that was mostly because I had morning sickness all the way through the middle of my third trimester. Everything I ate, even the smallest morsel of food, made me hurl. By the time the nausea finally began to subside, I was so huge and uncomfortable I couldn't eat or sleep. The only thing keeping me from being completely miserable was that I knew the baby was healthy because he was kicking me like a Kung Fu ninja.

We decided not to find out the baby's gender in advance this time, so on the day of my C-section we had two names picked out: Primrose for a girl or D'Artagnan for a boy. We had agreed on Primrose early on, but by my seventh month we still hadn't settled on a name for a boy. Then one day we were in our car listening to Citizen Cope, the one artist Joe and I are both equally devoted to. His music is very slow and mellow, like white man's reggae, and is perfect for lakeside life. While I was pregnant with Penelope, we had gone to a Citizen Cope concert, and backstage after the show he had blessed my belly. We were in the car and the song "D'Artagnan's Theme" came on and it reminded both of us of Joe's father, who had passed away a couple of years earlier from a rare blood disease. It's such a sad, beautiful song, and there's a line about "fading away" so we both felt that the name would be a loving tribute to his father. We decided that if we had a boy, Vincent, Joe's father's name, would the middle name and D'Artagnan would be the first.

The weekend before my C-section, Joe started having second thoughts about the name D'Artangnan, even though it was his idea in the first place. He kept making cracks like, "Dart the Fart, that's not going to happen." I get that he was worried about our son getting teased for having such an unusual name, but it was a name that was deeply meaningful to me. So even though his birth certificate says Grayson Vincent Gnoffo, our son will always be D'Artagnan to me.

Joe was the first to see our son when was born. When I heard him shout, "It's a boy!" (followed by the sound of our son crying as his healthy lungs filled with oxygen) I felt such an overwhelming sense of joy and relief. This time, I was able to hold my baby, skin-to-skin, right after he was born. They still had to sew me up from the C-section so it was only for a few moments, but my doctor assured me that when I came back from recovery my son would be in my room waiting for me. I kept asking, "There's nothing wrong with him? Really? He's

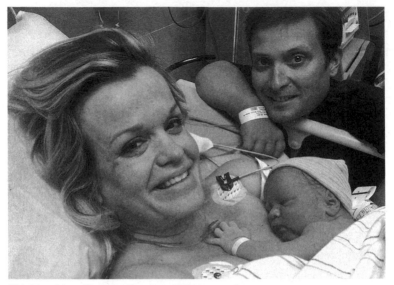

Skin-to-skin with baby Grayson (D'Artagnan).

healthy?" We had dealt with so many issues with Penelope, that it was hard to wrap my mind around the fact that I had just given birth to a healthy baby.

We knew right away D'Artagnan (I don't care what Joe says, that's his name) wasn't achon because his legs and head circumference were equal to an average-sized baby. We tested for pseudoachondroplasia at birth, but the results were inconclusive. There is a still a chance that he could have Joe's kind of dwarfism, but pseudo babies develop at an average rate until about the age of two, when cells start dying off and bone growth rapidly slows down. The only way to know for sure before then is for both Joe and D'Artagnan to have a blood panels done and to compare the two. We've decided not to do more testing and to just wait and see what happens with D'Art. It's not that insurance won't cover Joe's testing, (which they won't because

Penny meets her new little brother.

it's considered "elective"); it's more out of a fear that I will treat him differently if we find out he's little. I feel like not knowing if he's pseudo keeps me from subconsciously handicapping him as a parent. Joe and I just want to love D'Art, no matter what. We still monitor his health and physical wellbeing, but whether he turns out to be pseudo or average it's not going to change our love for him. Either way we will raise our son in a loving family and we will be there to support him through anything life throws his way—which is pretty much the definition of parenthood.

As an LP family, you are faced with so many obstacles so you just have to take on each challenge as it comes. Being born with dwarfism presents physical and emotional hurtles that no parent wants their child to have to go through, but bringing a life into the world comes with risk whether you're average or little; it's the quality of that life that truly matters.

CHAPTER FIFTEEN

REACH FOR THE STARS

When I was approaching the end of my pregnancy with D'Art-agnan, I was called in to interview with the producers of *Dancing with the Stars*. They asked me about my dance experience and how I would feel about competing on the show so soon after having a baby. I left that meeting thinking it could go either way. I knew there was a good possibility that they were nervous about having a little person perform on the show. I wasn't sure they were willing to take the risk, especially given the fact that my body wasn't going to be in peak performance condition.

When I was officially invited to be on Season 23 of *Dancing with the Stars*, it was a dream come true. The only problem was that rehearsals were to begin three weeks after my scheduled C-section and I was honestly terrified that I wouldn't be able to recover in time (because of the incision, you're not supposed to do any strenuous activity for six to eight weeks after delivery). I spoke with my doctor about what the risks would be for me to put myself into such a physically demanding situation while

my body was still healing and he told me that if I had been a dancer prior it would be one thing, but because I wasn't a professional dancer it was just an unknown. While he couldn't guarantee it wouldn't lead to complications, he didn't exactly say no either.

My entire life I had wanted the opportunity to perform at this level. I had been working so hard for so many years and right when I least expected it I was being offered the opportunity to finally show the world what I was capable of. I could either choose to play it safe or I could jump in with both feet and give it everything I had. I've never been one to play it safe. I knew there were risks, but I was less afraid of trying and failing than I was of losing the opportunity to realize a dream.

I have always been huge fan of *Dancing with the Stars* and just to be invited on the show was such an honor, but the fact that I would be the first little person ever to compete on the show was very overwhelming. I remember, asking the producers at one point during that first meeting, "Have the dancers ever refused to work with a partner after meeting them?" I was also worried about how the viewers would respond to me being on the show. My greatest hope was that I would change people's attitudes and preconceived notions about little people; my darkest fear was that I would end up being seen as a joke.

Going into the second week after my C-section, I was still barely walking. We lived on a hill so I decided to take the kids for a walk in the double stroller. I used to take Penny on this walk all the time with no issue, but now almost immediately I was exhausted and out of breath trying to push that stroller up this one tiny hill. I remember thinking, "If I can't do this, I'll definitely be eliminated in the first round." I wasn't even rehearsing yet and I was already in competition mode because of the pressure I felt to make a strong showing as a little person.

Two weeks after giving birth, I met my dance partner, Sasha Farber, for the first time when he came to my house for the big reveal. When I opened the door, I could tell from the look on his face that he had never met a little person before. He also had no clue who I was. Not only did he have to ask me my name when we met, he forgot it and then had to ask me again. I'm sure his inner dialogue was, "What kind of celebrity are you?" Once I knew I'd be working with Sasha, I felt a new pressure to live up to his previous partners, Snookie and Kim Fields, both of whom are incredible dancers. I felt a tremendous responsibility to keep up with them and I didn't want Sasha to feel he already had a losing partner.

I think the reality of what I was in for really hit me on the day that we met all the other contestants for the first time. We had all gathered at a soundstage in Los Angeles for an all-cast photo shoot. There was nothing specific that anyone said or did, but there was just this energy in the room when I walked in. I could feel that nobody was intimidated by me, and I wasn't being taken seriously. Between my Vegas odds (which had me eliminated in the second round, after Rick Perry) and the energy in the room that day, I felt underestimated and dismissed. In that moment, I felt like I was back in high school; it was Ms.

Crabapple and Premier Choir all over again. I realized that, for the first time since high school, I would be competing with average-sized people and that kicked up a lot of issues for me and chipped away at my confidence going in. I went from just being glad to be on the show to struggling to reconcile insecurities I didn't even know I had, with a sudden and overwhelming drive to kick ass and prove to everyone—not least of all myself—that I belonged in the competition.

During that first photo shoot Sasha didn't know anything about me and I'm pretty sure he was thinking he would be able to just lift me up and throw me around like a doll (I'm small so I must be light). I remember we were doing poses for the photo shoot, and when he picked me up into a lift, all of a sudden his calm face turned to total panic—like, *how am I going to lift this chick on a regular basis?* We rehearsed at a studio near my house for two weeks before the season officially began and, in the beginning, it was a lot of figuring out what boundaries to push with each other. I think Sasha was definitely scared at that first rehearsal; my arms don't extend fully straight, my knees pop in and out of socket, and I could barely walk in ballroom heels, much less dance. At first, he didn't want to hurt my feelings so he was very careful with his words, but towards the end of the day he finally had me switch into my tennis shoes and he was like, "Holy shit. We have a dancer."

It took a few weeks for Sasha and I to really connect. I feel like he thought I was a nice person and I was doing my job as a dancer, but he didn't necessarily love me as a human being until three or four weeks in. Once we broke the seal, and we developed the kind of trust and intuitive connection you need in a strong partnership, he was able to teach me how to modify certain steps to accommodate my shortcomings (pun intended) as a dancer. Because my left leg isn't completely straight I had to learn to overextend it; it's incredibly uncomfortable but it looks pretty. But the most important lesson I learned from Sasha was to forget about the competition and to focus on improving as a dancer from week to week.

You cannot imagine the fear, excitement, and adrenalin pumping through my body on the night of the season premier. Our first dance was the Jive, which is a very fast-paced, high-energy dance. As Sasha and I were standing onstage, waiting to perform that first night, my hands were ice cold—so I knew I was terrified. Before every dance the producers show a minute and twenty-second video, called a package, of whatever happened the week before. For days leading up to that moment, Sasha had warned me, "Whatever you do, don't listen to the package." If you watch it before a performance and see yourself crying or in conflict with your partner it can get inside your head and throw you off your game.

"Right now," I heard Tom Bergeron saying, "we have got the very first little person ever to compete on any *Dancing with the Stars*..."

That was the cue for our package. I clenched my eyes shut, covered my ears and started humming loudly to drown out the audio. When the package ended and our music began to play, it was almost like an out of body experience. You practice so much during the week that the choreography becomes embedded in your muscle memory, so your body kicks in even if your brain shuts down. The trick is to learn how to be in the moment so you can enjoy what you're doing. It reminded me of that feeling of being in show choir when I was a kid.

The choreography for our dance ended with Sasha spinning me around his body on the stage floor and then I popped up for

dramatic low dip in his arms. The moment we finished dancing Sasha picked me up into a huge bear hug. Joe, my brother, Tonya, and Elena were in the audience, and when I looked over at them they were on their feet, clapping and cheering. That's when I realized that the entire audience was standing and cheering for us too. Up to that moment I really had no idea how people would respond to me being on the show, so it was incredibly gratifying to feel that level of love and support right out of the gate. That was the moment where I started to feel, "Okay, I can do this."

Now it was time to hear what the judges had to say. Carrie Ann Inaba was the first judge to speak and the first thing she said to me was, "I didn't see a little person, I saw a huge star." She was my favorite judge because I felt like she understood my journey the most. She gave us a 7, but the other three judges (Len Goodman, Bruno Toniolo, and Julianne Hough) gave us 6s across the board, for total of 25 points.

The judge's scores were lower than I had hoped for. But Sasha said, "Don't think about the scores, just focus on what the judges had to say. Let's just move forward and come back better and stronger next week." After that first dance, something shifted inside me. I still felt that competitive drive to prove myself, but my confidence was growing and my biggest goal became to stay in the competition long enough to get to do all twelve dances.

Week two, we did the Quickstep and Julianne Hough said that my frame was the best she'd seen all night. Bruno Tonioli said my foot placement was "exactly on time and guided to perfection." I was learning and growing as a dancer and the other contestants were starting to take me seriously. Every week after that our scores improved and so did my technique. A lot of the struggles I had early on were related to the weight I had gained during pregnancy. My weight journey on *Dancing with the Stars* was crazy; I lost 30 pounds in 12 weeks.

For week five the theme was "Most Memorable Year." It just happened that it was a week after the three-year anniversary of my father's passing, so we decided to do a contemporary dance to commemorate his life. I remember during rehearsal I was told they needed me upstairs to do promos. I went up to the third floor and when I walked into the room, there was a photo on a massive TV screen of my dad, Bourn, and I on his speedboat with Lake Michigan in the background. My mind was instantly flooded with memories of all the summers and holidays Bourn

and I spent with our dad in Charlevoix, on the banks of Lake Michigan. Somehow, I pulled myself together long enough to get through the interview, but after that I was so emotional I couldn't even go back to rehearsal.

When the package aired before our dance that night, Sasha saw me tearing up. I remember, he grabbed me by the shoulders and said, "Sing something." My mind was blank, so I started singing the first song that came into my head, which for some reason was "Jingle Bell Rock." For the rest of my life, I will always think of that moment whenever I hear that song. Dancing that tribute to my father was one of the most bittersweet experiences of my life. He had always supported my choice to pursue a career as a performer and his belief in me never wavered. I never got the chance to say goodbye to my father or to thank him for his love and support, so in many ways that night gave me the closure that I had never had.

||||||||||||||||||||

THE SIXTEEN WEEKS THAT I spent rehearsing for and performing on *Dancing with the Stars* were some of the most physically challenging and emotionally rewarding of my entire life. I met some amazing people with whom I'll always have a bond because of the experiences we shared. You're in this intense situation and you get to know intimate things about people with whom you might never otherwise have crossed paths. After four or five weeks, they are the only other people who can relate to the physical and emotional roller coaster you're on. Some of them are on a different journey: they're there to become relevant again or to promote a show or an album. Some, like me, are there because they have something to prove. But, no matter the agenda, week after week each and every one of us poured our hearts and our souls into every single dance.

My favorite dance was the Charleston. We did a really fun flapper theme to "If My Friends Could See Me Now," with my name lit up in huge Broadway-style lights behind us. The Charleston requires extremely fast footwork, to the point where I lost my breath by its end, but it's such a technical dance that you feel super accomplished when you finish. One of my biggest goals of the competition was to get a perfect score. The next week, we made it to the semifinals. It was getting harder and harder the closer we got to the end and at this point the competition was steep. We had two numbers to learn, and we got 10s across the board for the Rhumba as well as for the Tango trio I danced with Sasha and Artem. Sadly, though, that was also the week we were eliminated.

We were going out with a double perfect score, but no matter what you have accomplished up to that moment, it is

still heartbreaking when they call your name for elimination. I don't know why I was eliminated, but I hope it was close and that I gave the final four contestants a run for their money. As much as I had I wanted to win, the bigger loss for me was that I was eliminated before I got to do every dance. That was a huge goal for me and it would have meant so much more to me than any trophy or dollar amount.

After we went through the press line, I took Sasha aside to thank him for being such an inspiration. It was a very intense, emotional moment because I felt like I had let him down. That season was the furthest that he had ever been in the competition, yet I felt like I failed him by not taking him all the way to the end. You could tell he was frustrated and sad, but he was super strong for me. After that I gave Joe a kiss and cried for a hot second. I could see the love and pride he felt for me written all over his face, which helped get me through the next 24 hours. After you get eliminated, there is a car waiting for you outside the studio and then you're whisked off to New York to be interviewed the following morning on *Good Morning America*.

And then it's over.

Back home, after the competition was over, if it hadn't been for Joe I probably would have been committed. I thought he was going to be relieved that I was home and our lives could get back to normal, but instead he was sympathetic and supportive. As happy as he was to have his wife back, Joe felt bad for me because he knew how badly I had wanted to make it all the way to the end of the competition. He reminded me of all that I had accomplished and that I had broken down barriers for little people everywhere. The one thing I never expected was the outpouring of support and respect I got from people both within the LP community and the general public. Instead of a trophy I walked away from the *Dancing with the Stars* with three hernias and a ripped diastasis, but I would do it all over again in a heartbeat.

||||||||||||||||||||||

NOW THAT I AM A parent, I have something even more important than ever to work for because I have a family to support and nurture. Now more than ever I have this drive to succeed, and to keep pushing forward in all directions. So many people think if you have the looks or the talent doors will open, but you have to put yourself out there and *make* it happen, and you have to be okay with failure. It's not, *what do I want to have handed to me?* But, *What do I want to go out and try next?* I always say, throw a lot of spaghetti at the wall and see what sticks. No one can know for sure how things will turn out; there's no crystal ball that can guarantee your dreams will come true, but if you don't say yes to opportunity then nothing will happen.

The experience of making it to the semifinals on *Dancing with the Stars* felt something like climbing the highest pyramid in the world. Each week I had felt that same sense of determination and accomplishment that I had experienced a year earlier as I pulled myself up each one of those 122 steps it took to get to the top of Ixmoja pyramid. We all have a path to follow and there will be times you will find huge obstacles in your way. You can back down and give up on your dreams, or you can choose to push yourself beyond what you thought you were capable. The bigger your dreams, the harder the road you will have to travel, but never let anything (least of all your size) stop you from pushing your way to the top.